.5o P

GH01007636

Pelican Books
Outside In ... Inside Out

Luise Eichenbaum and Susie Orbach are the founders of the Women's
Therapy Centre (London, 1976) and the Women's Therapy Centre
Institute (New York, 1981). As practising psychotherapists they are
involved in the post-graduate training of other mental-health
practitioners, sensitizing them to the issues related to the psychology
of women. The Women's Therapy Centre in London has received
local and national government funding and acts as a consultant to
local government mental-health committees. The material presented
in *Outside In ... Inside Out* was originally prepared for an in-service
training programme for psychiatrists, psychologists, psychotherapists,
psychiatric social workers and counsellors initially funded by the
Equal Opportunities Commission. In addition to their practice in
psychotherapy and teaching, the authors have given numerous talks,
lectures and seminars on the subject of women and mental health all
over the United Kingdom. Susie Orbach is the author of *Fat is a
Feminist Issue,* a self-help manual for compulsive eaters, and *Fat is a
Feminist Issue II.*

OUTSIDE IN ..

Luise Eichenbaum and Susie Orbach

INSIDE OUT

Women's Psychology:
A Feminist Psychoanalytic Approach

Penguin Books

Penguin Books Ltd, Harmondsworth, Middlesex, England
Penguin Books, 625 Madison Avenue, New York, New York 10022, U.S.A.
Penguin Books Australia Ltd, Ringwood, Victoria, Australia
Penguin Books Canada Ltd, 2801 John Street, Markham, Ontario, Canada L3R 1B4
Penguin Books (N.Z.) Ltd, 182–190 Wairau Road, Auckland 10, New Zealand

First published 1982

Copyright © Luise Eichenbaum and Susie Orbach, 1982
All rights reserved

Made and printed in Great Britain by
Richard Clay (The Chaucer Press) Ltd,
Bungay, Suffolk
Set in Monophoto Times

Contents

To all the women who came
to the Women's Therapy Centre
and shared so much with us.

Personal Introduction

On the morning of 6 April 1976 we deposited one hundred envelopes into the post-box outside Chalk Farm Tube station, London. Contained in each one was a letter and a leaflet announcing the opening of the Women's Therapy Centre in Islington on 8 April. The mailing went to women's groups, women's centres, doctors in the area, educational institutions, psychiatric clinics and national and local media. We were nervous and excited, eager to see the response. Later that day we took possession of the Centre's premises and, paint rollers in hand, kerchiefs on our heads, we spruced up two therapy rooms and an administrative office. Friends came to help and we chatted excitedly about our plans for the Centre. We were opening it, we said, because women wanted psychotherapeutic services that addressed women's needs, understood women's experience and supported women's struggles. As women who had contributed to a feminist-oriented therapeutic practice in the United States – both as clients and as therapists – we were eager to learn together and share our skills with women where we now lived. Sisters here talked about the absolute dearth of therapy services they could use and we felt that a centre could help redress this situation in many ways. First, it could offer psychotherapy from a feminist perspective; it would be a focus for those interested in women's psychology and could by its very existence highlight the shortcomings for and biases against women of existing treatment practices in mental hospitals, outpatient psychiatric clinics, analytic institutions, child-guidance clinics and so on.

Our training as therapists had come out of our involvement in the Women's Liberation Movement and the desire to understand and change the conditions of our lives. We had learned through the women's movement that our internal and external existence were entwined, that the outside world was inside us and that we needed to struggle on all fronts to produce social change.

During the following five years, the Centre moved to larger premises, began to get funded and was engaged in many activities. As the demand for the Centre's services grew so other women joined with us. The Women's Therapy Centre now has a staff of eleven therapists (some as part-time, some as full-time workers) – Sally Berry, Ellie Chaikind, Luise Eichenbaum, Sheila Ernst, Margaret Green, Sue Krzowski, Marie Maguire, Susie Orbach, Pam Smith, Alison Swan and Margot Waddell – as well as Mira Dana, Gill Holden and Jill Temple, who each came as a student for a year. In addition, the Women's Therapy Centre offers many groups and workshops run by group leaders who are not a part of the staff. The growth of the Centre has been propelled by the demand for its services and we have had a waiting list for both individual and group therapy since 1978, as a result of which we decided to use some of our resources by sharing what we were learning with other workers in the mental-health field.

Funded by the Equal Opportunities Commission we set up a ten-week in-service training programme for practising psychotherapists, psychiatric social workers, psychologists, psychiatrists and counsellors. The course meetings consisted of a lecture and discussion group, followed by small supervision groups led by us and by our colleague Sally Berry. This book is a refinement of the lectures we offered to the participants on those courses. The course led us to supervise the work of many psychotherapists. In this way we were to hear about the lives and psychologies of scores of women, adding to the experiences with our own clients. It is on this practice that we base our analysis of women's psychology.

As full-time members of the Women's Therapy Centre we have been very involved in giving talks and lecturing all over the United Kingdom. Everywhere we have gone we have met enthusiastic audiences receptive to the ideas presented in this book. What we were seeing in our clinical practice was confirmed by therapists all over the country, working in isolation.

Internally our learning has taken place in three specific ways. One has been the peer supervision group for the staff at the Women's Therapy Centre. Here we have discussed together what we were learning about women's psychology from the point of view of practice and technique. The group has shared a feminist perspective, although the routes into feminist psychotherapy were different for all of us and our group has always had some theoretical differences. The second context has been the staff study group where we have talked extensively without pressure and with great pleasure about our views on topics such as female sexuality, depression, psychological development, dreams, etc., always trying to start from our own personal and clinical experiences before moving on to reading. The third component of our learning has come from being a part of the office administration – seeing what people are wanting from the Women's Therapy Centre, by sharing in the answering of the hundreds of telephone calls and letters that arrive each week from all parts of the country.

The women who have come to the Women's Therapy Centre have, in their therapy, intimately shared with us parts of themselves. In so doing they have contributed to the creation of a clear and detailed picture of what is going on for all women psychologically within the present conditions of patriarchal social relations. We have found that most of the current theory and practice of psychotherapy is imprisoned within conventional patriarchal ideology and that women are being poorly served by present psychotherapeutic methods and approaches. The Women's Liberation Movement has now reached a level of development where it is possible to begin to articulate a radically new psychological theory of women based on feminist principles. The outline of a new understanding of the construction of a feminine psychology and the practice of feminist psychotherapy are the tasks of this book. It is for this reason that it has been necessary for us to present some of the material (Chapters 1 and 2) in a technical form.

Thanks are due to: our loving friends and colleagues at the Women's Therapy Centre; Frankie Liebe for high-quality help and enthusiasm in the critical last push; Helen Coleson for turning hieroglyphics into an exquisitely typed page; and Gillian Slovo for friendship and for reading and commenting on an early version of the text. Thanks also go to friends and family on both sides of the Atlantic for their love and support. Andy Friend and Joseph Schwartz's encouragement, love, support, criticism and enthusiasm were much felt, much needed and are deeply appreciated. Lastly, of course, this book owes much to our mothers Myrna Eichenbaum, Ruth Orbach and Anne Marie Sandler. In their own individual ways they are very important women for each of us.

We finish this book with joy, but also with sorrow, for it marks the end of a unique phase of our lives and of our relationship together. Our friendship has deepened through our time together at the Women's Therapy Centre and at the desk writing this book. Not only has our clinical practice served as data, so too has our relationship. We have struggled together as two women to develop a loving, equal relationship. This book represents a consolidation both of the work we have developed, hand in hand, over the past seven years and of our love for each other.

London, December 1980

Introduction to Feminist Psychotherapy

Locating Ourselves – the Women's Liberation Movement, Consciousness-raising Groups and the Beginnings of Feminist Psychotherapy

Our interest in women's psychology and feminist psychotherapy comes directly from our involvement in the Women's Liberation Movement. Women in the Movement formed consciousness-raising groups to create places in which to talk and discuss and uncover the stories of their lives as women. In the talking, the threads of common experience in the family, at school, with sex, at work, in the medical system and elsewhere began to knit together a picture of women's lives and of women's oppression. Women discovered that they shared feelings of powerlessness and rage, a sense of themselves as less than whole people, of frustration and under-development; they had common experiences of being led into specific roles and activities, of being discriminated against, of being limited in sexual expression and restricted in many areas of life and development. The consciousness-raising groups reflected the skills that women had learned well: how to listen and how to talk with each other, how to empathize and how to give emotional support.

In the consciousness-raising group women filled in the pieces of the jigsaw and began to construct their view of how society makes a woman a second-class citizen. We began to see the social basis of our individually experienced oppression. Each new idea and action was thought about and worked through. There was always an attempt to understand private lives, individual thoughts and individual actions from the vantage point of the *fact* of the overall oppression of women.

As the Women's Liberation Movement grew, so did its impact on society. As feminists went into the schools and hospitals to change education and medical policy, they joined with sympathizers within those institutions who were raising issues pertinent to the experience of women. Psychology, psychiatry and psychoanalysis were no less confronted by feminism than were other institutions of patriarchal power. Spearheaded by Phyllis

Chesler's illuminating study of women and the mental-health establishment [1][1], the Mental Patients Liberation Front, the Radical Therapy Collective in Cambridge, Mass. [2] and the actions of professionals who fought to withdraw the psychopathological designation of homosexual individuals seeking treatment for distress not related to their sexual orientation, the whole mental-health field was turned upside down. Two widely quoted studies, Pauline Bart's work on 'Depression in Middle-Aged Women' [3] and Broverman *et al*.'s 'Sex-Role Stereotypes in Clinical Judgements of Mental Health' [4], focused on two fundamental issues related to women and mental health. The Bart study discussed how the definition of mental health derives from 'feelings of well-being dependent on a positive self-concept' and how the internalization of the female role denies women the possibility of a positive self-concept. The Broverman study illustrated how psychology as a discipline and therapy contribute to and maintain sexist attitudes in the clinical treatment of women. Meanwhile, at the twenty-ninth International Psychoanalytic Congress in London in July 1975 [5] the Freudians held a dialogue on Freud and female sexuality which in itself demonstrated the impact of the Women's Liberation Movement.

The roots of feminist psychotherapy are in the consciousness-raising group. The Women's Liberation Movement brought the psychology of women into direct focus and provided the theoretical starting-point for the development of a psychotherapy for women from a feminist perspective. There are four major links between the consciousness-raising process and feminist psychotherapy. The first of these is that the Women's Liberation Movement asserted that personal life is a political affair. This was, of course, a direct challenge to the progressive left-wing movements of the sixties, which saw concern with personal matters as individualistic. Within the consciousness-raising group each person's experience, each woman's life story was a matter of interest. We understood that through listening to an individual's experience we could draw a much richer picture of how society was put together. Sexual politics provided an understanding of how society works both at an ideological level and at a material level and deepened the understanding the left had of human experience. The Women's Liberation Movement built an analysis of society founded on the nuts and bolts of individual life experience. It enlarged and challenged previous understanding of the social, economic and political basis of society.

The psychotherapy process is similarly concerned with the details of individual experience. Through the in-depth analysis of an individual's conscious and unconscious life, psychoanalytic psychotherapists have

1. Notes are printed on pages 115–23 below.

theorized about the workings of society [6], for the investigation of a person's psyche reveals the ensemble of social relations.

The second link between the consciousness-raising group and psychotherapy is the focus on the family. The post-war mythical family, as portrayed by the media, is one in which father is the breadwinner and works outside the home and mother works contentedly inside the home, raising the children, smoothly oiling the wheels of domesticity and providing emotional nurturing. Even if our own family did not fit this image (for example, if one parent was absent, or father was not the breadwinner, or both parents worked outside the home), it was nevertheless organized on sexual lines, with women and men having clearly defined roles and responsibilities. In the consciousness-raising group and in psychotherapy we discover the importance of the family in shaping our own childhoods and in determining our experience of becoming adult. We focus on relationships within the family and the expectations, affections, rewards, and restrictions which influenced our behaviour and attitudes as little girls and subsequently as women.

The family was our first social world. In it we first learnt our sexual roles. Feminists have taken up the history of the family and shown how, in its present form, it is a recent development [7]. The transformation from a feudal economy to a modern capitalist state has gone hand in hand with changes in the family unit which have led to the sexual division of labour within the family and the relegation of women to a subordinate position as wife and mother. A feminist psychotherapy is interested in how the social practices of a given culture are transmitted to its members and how the individual internalizes the power relations, the sex-roles and the psycho-dynamics of the family.

The third link between consciousness-raising and psychotherapy is that both processes are concerned with the emotional life of the individual. In the consciousness-raising group women came to feel more comfortable, less ashamed of the strong feelings that they were beginning to discover inside them. Feelings of anger, pain, depression and sadness were seen as understandable expressions of a woman's psychological experience. This kind of discovering and untapping of taboo emotions is very much a part of the psychotherapeutic process. Given the basic principle of the validity of emotional life, both consciousness-raising and psychotherapy look beyond the content and construction of particular emotions; for example, romantic feelings or passionate feelings are not taken at face value but are scrutinized for clues to understand their derivation and to grasp why such feelings are so important in the individual and collective lives of women.

The fourth link centres around the topic of sexuality, previously a taboo subject. From Freud onwards psychotherapists [8] have been engaged in the study of sexuality at an emotional, philosophical and political level. In consciousness-raising groups, women began to try to understand what sexuality was – how it was formed, what it meant in our lives, what kinds of dissatisfactions (and satisfactions) we had, whether sexuality was something sacred, whether sexual relationships were in some sense also political relationships and so on. In the consciousness-raising group we tried to understand women's sexual fantasies. That in turn shed light on women's sexual experience [9]. In addition we looked at heterosexuality and lesbianism, and produced not only a critique of a heterosexual society but also stressed the importance of understanding the political relationship between women and their sexuality.

Women who participated in consciousness-raising groups experienced enormous changes in their lives. Consciousness-raising transformed the way we saw the world. We saw aspects of our day-to-day experience from an entirely fresh perspective. We were often angry and just as often exhilarated.

After the first few years of involvement in consciousness-raising groups (and political activity outside the groups), because of the profound changes that had taken place the limitations of the consciousness-raising groups then emerged. We were in a situation where consciousness was changing tremendously fast, as was the pattern of women's lives in terms of their relationships at home, at work, with their children and families, but where society as a whole was not keeping pace with the kinds of changes women were demanding. Women felt that they had changed a lot and yet society had not; i.e. material changes did not reflect changes in consciousness. So the consciousness-raising group was the first step in the process of understanding and change. Because society was not altering radically enough to consolidate the changes in consciousness, we found that many aspects of our behaviour instead of being continually challenged and reshaped seemed to stand still. Change of behaviour and feelings was at times excruciatingly difficult. We may have believed that women should now all feel assertive and entitled; we may have believed women should be independent, not possessive or insecure; but these emotional responses did by and large seem to be unconscious and repetitive.

A second difficulty, which we can analyse in retrospect, was that precisely because the consciousness-raising groups were so emotionally charged – everything being so new, exciting and frightening – feelings between members in the groups were often not handled very well. Feelings of envy, competition, anger and love emerged and were so powerful that the groups could sometimes neither contain nor cope with them. So women in these groups had to ask: How do we change what is so deeply rooted in us? How can I change how I feel? How can I understand things that are operating on an unconscious level? We, together with many women, found ourselves looking to psychotherapy to see if it could give us access to some of these answers.

The study of psychoanalysis proved problematic for many feminists at this time, because of the anti-Freud bias of early stages of sections of the Movement [10]. Freudian psychoanalytic practice was seen to be explicitly reactionary in relation to its understandings of women's psychology and femininity. There were some feminists who believed psychoanalysis did have something to offer, but at that time they were in the minority. Women in the United States were drawn to humanistic psychology, the growth-movement psychotherapies, which seemed to offer a way for women to discover parts of themselves that were repressed, split off or in opposition to the stereotype view they held of themselves [11]. The techniques of gestalt therapy, transactional analysis, psychodrama, assertion training and so on were accessible and could be learnt fairly quickly. These therapeutic techniques offered three things: first, they held out the possibility that individuals could get in touch with their feelings more speedily than through psychoanalytical methods; second, they supported individuals to act on their own behalf; and third, they demystified the process of psychological change.

After several years of practice based on these tenets, outstanding innovations were introduced, mostly within group context [12]. Women were feeling and being more assertive, getting in touch with a range of emotions previously defined as taboo for women, and feeling and acting differently in the world. However, persistent stumbling-blocks to emotional change led us to turn more attention to unconscious processes, and to the serious study of psychoanalytic, psychotherapeutic practice. The turn to psychoanalysis came from our understanding of the critical nature of early family experience in forming our psychology. At that time, humanistic psychology, working in the here and now, seemed to limit the satisfactory exploration of family history and the unconscious. Many feminists were already using certain psychoanalytic tools in their work and incorporating them into psychotherapeutic practice. In turning to psychoanalysis, we as feminist psychotherapists recognized the importance of Freud's discovery of the unconscious and the existence of a psychic life that was a powerful determinant in the politics of everyday experience. At the same time, we rejected a view of a 'self' conceived outside culture and began to see how individual reality and personality is shaped by the material world. We see the unconscious as the intra-psychic reflection of our present child-rearing and gender relations [13].

Our work has coalesced with another trend within the Women's Liberation Movement: the exploration of the mother–daughter relationship through analytic means. New lines of development do not emerge in isolation. For several years there have been consciousness-raising groups, therapy workshops, and writings – most notably those of Nancy Chodorow [14], Nancy Friday [15], Adrienne Rich [16], and Signe Hammer [17] – exploring the meaning and impact of the mother–daughter relationship. Drawing on the disciplines of psychoanalysis, sociology, social psychology, mythology and literary criticism, these explorations provide a rich background in which our theory and practice are cradled.

I Psychological Development

From the moment of birth, babies enter a social world, not yet with fully developed personalities but with the capacity to become a part of human culture. All their subsequent experiences of physical and emotional growth are part of the process of becoming a person in a particular social context. The first month of a baby's life may be thought of as a continuation of life within the uterus. The infant still seems to live in an enclosed world preoccupied with its own physical sensations. The satisfaction of its physical needs – hunger, urinating, passing wind, warmth and physical contact – all take place within this new womb. The baby floats in a world of new sounds, smells and tactile stimulation. From the sixth week on we begin to see tremendous changes in the baby. Its eyes focus and connect with people around it. It begins to explore itself and its environment in new ways. It touches its toes and hands, its mother's breasts and people's hands, as if to grasp the objects which inhabit its world. It experiences itself and mother as being within the same physical and psychological world inside a common boundary [1]. It does not have a sense of itself as a defined separate person.

The first two years of life are the most important time for the development of the inner core of the person, the ego, the psyche and the personality [2]. What makes each person unique is the particular way in which each personality – each person's ego – is formed. Ego development takes place from birth and the food for the developing ego is contact in a human relationship. The infant has a *primary* need for human contact. Without such contact babies die [3].

In the first months of life the mother is the most constant person in the infant's world. She is the anchor, the mediator for the baby's experiences. The baby relies on mother's empathy, attentiveness and understanding to survive. Now outside the womb the baby has a sort of psychological umbilical cord with the mother. This invisible connection of emotion experienced and transmitted from adult to infant feeds the developing ego of the infant. This is not to say that the baby is an empty receptacle waiting to be filled,

17

but rather that there is an intricate process in which the caring environment responds to the baby's needs. Babies are very expressive before the acquisition of language. Through a range of cries, noises and facial expressions the baby communicates to those around it. A baby's communications and the responses to them are necessary and important aspects of the process of ego development. It is through these communications that the baby makes its needs known and has them attended to or not, as the case may be.

The baby comes to feel its ability to have an impact on its world. It experiences itself in relationship to those outside of it. When the baby smiles and gurgles it may be acknowledging the impact of others upon it, of the pleasure they provide which the baby feels. Giggles, gurgles and cries are communications in a relationship.

The caring, love, attention and security the mother provides are all experienced and taken in by the infant. Part of appropriate empathy and nurturance is the ability of the caretaker to provide a structure, a containment and a sense of boundaries for the baby. All during this early period mother is empathizing with the baby's needs. Because the baby is in the process of developing its own sense of self and does not yet have any boundaries, mother must bring the boundaries into the relationship. That is, mother must relate to the baby as a separate person. Various forms of saying 'no' or setting limits for the baby are not necessarily rejections or withholdings. They are necessary demonstrations of limits for the baby which provide a safety net and a sense of containment.

Satisfying and 'good' experiences are the threads that weave good ego development. That is to say, the consistent love, appropriate nurturance and setting of boundaries create a sense of psychological well-being within the infant. These experiences promote a positive sense of self, a self-love, and a sense of internal substance, a feeling that the world is basically safe.

The existential phenomenon of realizing yourself as a separate person, as a subject in the world, comes about through a process of secure, positive, 'healthy' ego development. Through the baby's earlier interactions and the 'taking-in' of others relating to it, the baby develops a self and personality. It embodies the love, care and security from those around it and comes to feel visible and substantive. In the period from six to eighteen months the sense of mother and others as 'other' – as external people – develops. Communications and responses to the baby all contribute to this weaving process of the psychological birth of a new person. In the early months, therefore, the mother allows the infant to be totally connected, merged. Then, being in tune with the baby's changing needs, mother lets go as the baby takes its first steps to separate and become its own person. During this

process, called separation-individuation [4], children are continually establishing a clearer sense of themselves. They begin to test their own
independence. The child's future sense of adventure, curiosity and taste for
life are strongly affected by the attitudes, conscious and unconscious, of
the people around her or him at this time.

The earlier experience of life – that of being merged with mother, of the
world and baby all being one – now changes and there is, for the baby, an
outside and a sense of 'I'. The baby experiences its own existence. It now
explores its hands, toes etc. in a new way. There is a new curiosity as baby
touches and looks at the faces of others around it.

When and if secure ego development occurs, we see the baby beginning
to maintain a sense of itself even when its caretaker is not present. The
baby now embodies the love and care of the other. Mother no longer is the
only person with a sense of self within this relationship. This means that
the baby does not experience a loss of itself when mother leaves the room
[5]. It experiences, with varying degrees of upset and acceptance, the tem-
porary loss of mother. It recovers its equilibrium readily. The baby has a
sense of itself apart from, *separate from*, mother. The experience of continued love and caring is critical to this sense of security within the baby.
The infant, secure in the love of its caretaker, feels that mother will return
and the caring will continue. The love is an invisible thread between baby
and mother so that although they are physically apart there remains a
reliable connection between them.

When secure ego development does not occur the process of separation
is modified. The baby may feel insecure in its world. It does not experience
its own separate identity. To the extent that its needs go unmet it will not
be able to achieve psychological separation because it is still yearning and
still in need of the psychological umbilical cord with mother. It has not
had sufficient nurturance to stand separate. Achieving a clear sense of
psychological separation is extremely problematic because we know that in
these first two years all babies are bound to have frustrating and upsetting
experiences as well as nurturing ones. Frustrated or upsetting experiences
need not be caused by inadequate caring or attention. For an infant the
experience of hunger, even if it is only for two or three minutes, can be
distressing. A baby's upset does not necessarily signify mother's withholding or lack of caring. The infant's experience of feeling hunger and then
expressing distress is a necessary communication from the baby to the
world. The response the baby gets to its communication is an experience
that is important in feeling its impact within its environment. In so far as
the baby's needs are responded to and the caretaker can connect and relate
with the baby, separation is more likely to be possible. Where the

caretaker has difficulty in connecting to and relating to the baby, that absence of connection makes the process of separation by baby less likely.

In whatever way the mother responds, a crucial factor is that the baby experiences her or his upset in relation to mother. This factor is of enormous importance in the developing psychology of the infant and later the child.

The developing infant is, at a certain level, helpless. Its communications will not always be understood and it cannot control the actions of its caretaker. On the psychological and physical levels it is utterly vulnerable and dependent. Although the infant is in this sense passive, there is enormous activity of an internal nature. Its embryonic psyche takes the only path available and transfers the difficult situation to the world of inner reality where it can exercise more control. In other words, there is at the same moment an internal experience of an 'outside' situation. The external situation may be out of the infant's control completely and therefore not alterable, but its internal experience is malleable and adjustable. In its internal world the child juggles with relationships so that they provide more satisfaction. In this sense the child has an *internal* life, an unconscious life, of relationships. Because these relationships are stripped of their truly interactive nature they are essentially relations with *objects*.

This dynamic of taking something into the inner world can be easily understood, perhaps, if we think of the way in which we, as adults, try to cope with upsetting situations by replaying and rearranging them in our heads. We imagine the situation in a different, more satisfactory way in our day-dreams. We come up with creative solutions. So it is for the child. During this early process of ego development, the infant is internalizing the distressing experience and attempting to change it. But alas, this attempt fails. The inner world is always interacting with the outside world, with actual, real people. The internal construction of object relations is thus modified by these actual experiences. The unsatisfying experiences that occur in relation to mother then find their expressions in a particular reflection of her in the infant's inner world. Mother as a disappointing person comes to be split into two. These two aspects of mother symbolize the known and longed-for giving mother and the known and deeply disappointing mother. Both these representations of mother are repressed in the unconscious. In the inner economy of the infant's embryonic psyche, the unsatisfying object continues to frustrate her or his needs at the same time as it whets them with the potential of satisfaction. In the external world, however, if the needs continue to be unmet, the infant gets hungrier and hungrier for what it is needing and wanting. The outside world appears less nourishing. Inside, the infant is desperate.

Let us look at Ruth to illustrate this process and see how these experiences appear in the following ways in the psychology of the adult. Ruth has had some good experiences with her mother early on and throughout her life. However her mother has, in fact, a great deal of difficulty in giving warmth and love and so appears to be a cold, ungiving, teasing person. Because Ruth has not received sufficient nurturance she is unable to achieve a psychological separation from her mother. She still feels connected to her, entwined with her and in need of her in essential ways.

The way Ruth has come to cope with the disappointing and upsetting experiences with her mother is to control them and 'forget' the pain of her unmet needs. She tries to transform the image of her mother, because acceptance of the reality is too painful. The unconscious processes involved are as follows. Ruth takes into herself – very early in her psychological development – the frustrating experiences of her mother. She then represses and, in her psyche, divides this unsatisfying person (object) into two. One part, with the promise of attentiveness, continues to enthrall her; the other part, which is unresponsive, continually disappoints her and makes her feel rejected. We see that each time Ruth is going to visit her mother she is hoping on an unconscious level that this time mother will be different – this time her mother will be the way Ruth needs and wants her to be, warm, loving, etc. Ruth yearns for her mother to give her the acceptance and the love she so desperately wants. She craves this acceptance so that she can finally feel good within herself and become a separate person. But inevitably the visits are painful. Ruth feels disappointed and unsatisfied. This knowledge continues to hurt and plague her. Ruth wants to have a different experience with her mother. Her inner world is in ascendancy. She cannot accept the disappointment, the fact that mother is cold and ungiving. It is intolerable. She again makes mother potentially satisfying, and so the internal split of mother is perpetuated. At a conscious level Ruth feels mother should, could, be doing more. She still wants so much and feels bad for the wanting. Ruth's psychological experience illustrates the translation and continuity between infant and adult psychic life.

An adult may consciously feel that her or his needs are insatiable and may be overwhelmed by feelings of self-dislike and greed. Feeling and expressing anger towards those who disappoint or fail to meet one's needs is problematic, for if it is expressed there is a fear that one will be further rejected and abandoned.

Ruth unconsciously turns her anger for mother against herself and feels that there is something wrong with her needs – and *therefore herself*.

Because Ruth is still holding on to and connected to her mother, and still wanting so much from her, the anger seems to be too dangerous a weapon. Instead Ruth feels that it is her own fault that her mother cannot give – she feels it is because she is too hungry and needy. Ruth comes to deny this needy part of herself. In denying the need, she is forced to cut off a part of herself, hiding it from the outer world and relationships – hiding it from herself – in other words it becomes repressed. This hidden part of the person now withdraws into an inner world and experiences a sense of futility and hopelessness. (This split in the ego has been called the schizoid split [6].) The possibility of connecting to the loved one (the potentially satisfying relationship) seems further and further away as one feels trapped within oneself. In adult life most people, to some extent, feel that an essential part of their personality is hidden from others: they often feel that the part of them that is in the world is somewhat inauthentic and fraudulent because there is a subconscious awareness of this unintegrated part. The repression of these aspects of the personality creates a form of alienation, in which one feels apart from and cut off from other people. Of course, the repression is only partially successful and aspects of the hidden part emerge indirectly.

This leads us to another brick in the construction of the ego – the defences. In order to protect this hidden part, the psyche creates defences. An example of a defence in Ruth's psychology is embodied in her idea that she does not want anything at all from her mother. Her attempt at not wanting, and appearing to others as not wanting, is in fact a defence against its very opposite, her tremendous feelings of neediness and yearning for nurturance from her mother. Defences are unconscious protective mechanisms in the struggle not to feel pain, anger, loss – unpleasant feelings that are very frightening. Defences operate in two ways; self-protective ways as well as self-destructive ones. For as the defence attempts to keep out rejections and disappointments from the outside world, at the same time it can prevent care and nurturance from coming in. So the hidden part of the ego develops defences to protect it from anticipated hurt.

The defences also protect others, the needed and loved ones, from this hidden part which is felt to be destructive, devouring and bad. Defences may indeed act against the interests of the person in that they can push people away or keep them at a distance, and possibly aid in the promotion of unsatisfactory relationships which only reinforce the anticipated fear of rejection or the feeling of the impossibility of having contact in relationship.

It is important to remember that defences have developed in the first place as protection within distressing relationships or situations. In one sense defences are creative mechanisms of human beings to protect themselves psychologically. At the same time defences create distance and separateness from others. These defences are psychological adaptations arising out of fear, upset and a defensive stance in relation to the world. In the first two years of life the psychological birth of the human infant entails the experience of contact and the taking-in of nurturance from the caretaker. As we have seen, the delicacy of this relationship inevitably contains enormous pleasure, intimacy, sensuality, upset, distance, frustration and difficulty. As the ego develops it copes with the difficult aspects of the relationship by splitting; internalizing the bad object and creating defences.

Father's presence is also reflected in the developing personality of the baby. Fathers for the most part have less interaction with small infants, being somewhere outside the orbit of mother and infant [7]. Before the process of separation the father may be experienced within the infant's world, but it is the mother who is the consistent presence. Father is with the infant far less and so his smell, touch and sounds are not the familiar ones of mother. Just as father experiences his wife and himself as the couple and the baby as the third person in a triangle, the baby experiences itself with mother and may feel father to be the third person, the outsider, the stranger.

As the baby develops, realizes its separateness and becomes aware of the people and things around it, so it now looks to father with new curiosity. The infant observes and tries to take in a sense of this very different person. Fathers play an important part in the baby's attempt to separate from mother. For the baby boy, father is 'other' than mother and like him. The boy identifies with father and utilizes this to separate himself further from mother. He may emulate and imitate father as the role model for whom he is to become.

For the little girl, father is 'other', whereas the little boy experiences himself as 'other' from the moment of birth because mother relates to him as 'other'. The little girl, being of the same gender as mother, has not come to experience intimacy with an 'other'. Her original intimacy is homosexual. Feeling herself to be 'other' with father aids the little girl in her developing sense of separateness [8].

She can feel boundaries with father because of his 'otherness' that she may not feel with mother. Father's personality is different from mother's and so for both the girl and boy infant the relationship with father, the quality of caring, loving, withholding, distance etc. will also come to play an important part in the developing ego of the baby. An older brother may also serve as an 'other' for the little girl. Brother is not the same as

23

mother and the little girl may move close to the brother in her attempts to separate from mother. This sense of 'otherness' based upon sexual differences is central to psychological development.

As the baby makes its steps towards its psychological birth as a separate person, it learns that people fall into two categories, female and male. By the age of one, children can point to male and female figures as either mum or dad and at eighteen months can recognize themselves as either female or male [9].

The baby's developing personality is highly influenced by this early sense of gender identity and the assimilation of either a feminine or a masculine gender. As the baby develops it comes to know itself as either a girl or a boy. When a baby is born there is a recognition on the part of its family of its place and role in the world based upon its sex. In the most minor and major ways every communication and contact with the baby is imbued with a sense of gender and people have profoundly different expectations for girls and boys, which the child learns. In all cultures one of the primary laws is that of sexual categories of masculine and feminine. People are not seen to be simply human, or even human with differing sexual, biological characteristics of masculinity and femininity. In our culture, as in many other cultures, these characteristics are not equal [10]. For instance 'brave', 'strong', 'rugged', 'capable', 'confident' are examples of valued masculine characterizations while 'petite', 'weak', 'helpless', 'giving', 'pretty', 'dainty', 'demure' are prized feminine ones. Infants then, are anticipated in gender categories. Will it be a boy? Is it a girl? All those who relate to a baby will have specific expectations for a girl and for a boy, which a child learns.

Recently attempts have been made to separate the biological, psychological and cultural aspects of personality development. Before the emergence of the Women's Liberation Movement, there was a widely held view that women's psychology derived from their biology, that is, their reproductive function, and men's psychology from their biology. Recent studies on gender identity show that by the time a child is two years old its gender identity is firmly fixed [11]. Money and Erhardt [12], psychologists who have studied hermaphrodites, that is people who possess mixed sexual characteristics, argue that in order to understand concepts of masculinity and femininity we must separate the biological basis from the cultural. Their work shows very clearly that the ideas we hold about femininity and masculinity relate to the cultural practices of a given society and not to biological imperatives. Their research shows that humans are not born with a masculine or a feminine psychology, but that women's psychology and men's psychology are fashioned to fit in with what is thought of as masculine and feminine. They argue that apart from biological sex – i.e.

women's capacity to menstruate, to conceive, to give birth and to lactate, and men's capacity to impregnate – the attributes we associate with femininity and masculinity are cultural constructions.

Money and Erhardt's work showed that those hermaphrodites who are raised as males despite the lack of a penis, and those raised as females despite the lack of ovaries and even with the development of male secondary sexual characteristics, saw themselves as male or female, and organized their world-view within masculine or feminine perspectives based on gender assignment. When these hermaphrodites discovered secondary sexual characteristics of the opposite sex, this did not create a gender-identity confusion in them, but a desire to erase the opposite sex manifestation. If biology were at the root of masculinity and femininity these individuals would have suffered a severe gender-identity crisis. Instead, what they were very eager to do was to maintain themselves, since they saw themselves as either male or female, as women or as men, and to get rid of any physical characteristics that did not relate to that gender.

Along with this knowledge of oneself as a girl or a boy goes, as we know, a series of behaviours, feelings and actions that are deemed appropriate for a girl or a boy. The stereotyping of sex roles means that boys and girls feel uncomfortable, awkward and out of place if they are involved in activities that have been presented to them as out of bounds for their sex. Although sex-role stereotyping is universal, it varies from culture to culture, and the rigidity of each child's immediate environment varies. As a result many girls will grow up with the idea that it is perfectly acceptable for women to become engineers or to be assertive, or not to be linked to a mate and so on, while other women's sexual identity would be threatened if they were to perform typically masculine tasks and jobs. But however varied the child's environment there will be activities that are seen to be definitely outside the child's and later the adult's realm because of his or her sex. They will feel wrong. The construction of personality then is intricately linked to a person's gender identity.

This is an extremely important starting-point for us, not only in so far as it sweeps away the cobwebs of biological determinism but in the light it sheds on the importance of social experience in human life, particularly early social life. In contrast to the views of many psychologists, we would stress the importance of culture in shaping the needs, desires and psychic life of women and men. *Femininity and masculinity, then, are psychological entities within a social context.* Gender identity and a sense of self emerge together and reflect the prevailing culture and pattern of parenting. It is within this context that we ask the question – what is a feminine psychology?

References on Development Psychology

Balint, A., *The Early Years of Life: A Psychoanalytic Study*, New York, 1954.
Balint, M., *Primary Love and Psycho-analytic Technique*, London, 1965.
Fairbairn, W. R. D., *Psychoanalytic Studies of the Personality*, London, 1952.
Freud, A., *The Ego and the Mechanisms of Defense*, 1936.
Guntrip, H., *Schizoid Phenomena and Object Relations Theory*, London, 1968.
Hartmann, H., *Ego Psychology and the Problem of Adaptation*, New York, 1958.
Jacobson, E., *The Self and the Object World*, New York, 1964.
Klein, M., *The Psycho-analysis of Children*, London, 1932.
Klein, M., *Love, Guilt and Reparation*, London, 1937.
Klein, M., *Envy and Gratitude*, London, 1957.
Mahler, M., *et al.*, *The Psychological Birth of the Human Infant*, New York, 1975.

Women's Ego Development

The girl, because of her deep emotional tie with her mother and her recognition of her as being the same, is driven to choose her as a model and to reproduce this model faithfully in herself. The mother's behaviour, her reactions, the relationship between the girl and the mother, and between the mother and every other member of the family, all indicate the values to which the mother herself responds (through the unconscious process of identification). The essence of the mother penetrates the girl and is absorbed by her. This means that everything depends on what the mother is like. But however exceptional she may be, she remains a woman; a being with lower social value than the man's, for whom tasks of secondary importance are reserved. If this is the model the girl must interiorize, girls have little reason to rejoice.

   – Elena Gianini Belotti, *Little Girls* (p. 59)

The Mother–Daughter Relationship

The Women's Liberation Movement has given us a totally new way to understand women's psychology. As millions of women in the 1960s and 1970s rebelled against an impossible social role, first in one-to-one conversations, then meeting together in consciousness-raising groups, organizations, marches and protest actions, an understanding of the inner dimensions of women's social position has slowly emerged. Women examined their life experiences together and named the system that was oppressing them: patriarchy. Through the process of trying to change our society we made ourselves conscious and we began to develop an understanding of how social expectations were affecting us on a psychological level. We discovered how we felt about the obligations and restrictions we experienced on a daily basis. This discovery on a feeling level thrust us into discovering the vital connections between the social world that women inhabit and the inner private world that governs us in the deepest reaches of our personalities.

The simple fact, previously hidden by ideological overgrowths, is that women do have a social existence. And it is out of our experience in society that an understanding of women's psychology must be sought; not, as is usually taught, the other way around, whereby women's social roles are seen to flow naturally from women's psychology, a psychology invariably seen as determined by biology. The Women's Liberation Movement taught us how much of our actions and feelings was caught up in trying to cope with society's rules about what and who women should be. So the development of a new understanding of women's experiences rests on bringing into bold relief exactly what these rules are.

Woman's primary social role is to be wife and mother. Man's primary social role is to be the family breadwinner. This is the defining edge of all female experience: that the young woman will grow up; that she will meet a man who will be her partner in life; that he will, until very recently at least, look after her economically; that she in turn will bear children and make a home for them and for the man. These features of women's social role, growing into a woman (with attendant conditioning), finding a mate, becoming a wife, learning to take care of babies, and making a home involve extensive social preparation. They are not inevitable consequences of women's biology. In order to find a man a woman has to present herself in a certain way. She has to develop her sexuality along particular lines; she has to create an image of herself that a man will find pleasing. This is a complex social matter, not at all a straightforward 'natural' process.

In the course of being a wife, the woman will be required to set up house, organize all the household matters as smoothly and efficiently as she can, be a helpmate to her husband, making sure that all the things he needs in his daily life are available – that his meals are cooked, that his clothes are at the ready and so forth. Being a wife is like having a job, but the training for this job is not overt, nor is the job itself valued.

Soon after marriage there is pressure on a woman to have a child. Being a wife and becoming a mother are so deeply entwined that a woman who has been married for several years and has not had a child feels herself to be somewhat odd and senses the curiosity and concern of others about her childlessness.

The woman as mother must *learn* how to take care of babies, change their nappies, feed them, respond to them emotionally, and help them to develop as well-adjusted children into the very same social sex-roles that she grew up with. In the first stages of their lives she will be responsible for arranging appropriate activities for them and structuring the life of the whole family. She will be expected to deal with the emotional realm of family life, keeping contacts with and having knowledge about the various branches of her own and her husband's extended family. Emotions will be her concern.

The first psychological demand that flows from a woman's social role is that she must *defer* to others, follow their lead, articulate her needs only in relation to theirs. In essence, she is not to be the main actor in her own life. As a result of this social requirement, women come to believe that they are not important in themselves for themselves. Women come to feel that they are unworthy, undeserving and unentitled. Women are frequently self-deprecating and hesitant about their own initiatives. They feel reluctant to speak for themselves, to voice their own thoughts and ideas, to act on their own behalf. Being pushed to defer to others means that they come to undervalue and feel insecure about themselves, their wants and their opinions. A recognition of a woman's own needs can therefore be complicated and a process occurs in which women come to hide their desires from themselves.

This social requirement of deferring may lead a woman to feel like she is a shadow. A tragic aspect of women's individually experienced inequality is that she is isolated in her feelings of inadequacy and lack of confidence. She cannot imagine that other women have similar feelings. This painful comparison further isolates her and leaves her with bad feelings about herself. She may imagine that other women's lives are more fulfilling and wonder how they achieve it.

The second requirement of woman's social role is that she must always be *connected* to others and shape her life according to a man. A woman's status will derive from that of her mate. Indeed her very sense of self and well-being may rely on their connection. A woman may look to a man to complete her life, to give her an identity and a purpose. Women come to feel odd, not right within themselves, perhaps a little at a loss, if they are not connected to a man. Our culture does not have a positive image of a woman on her own. It is never seen as a choice. It always appears as something that befalls her and engenders sympathy. The word for a woman on her own is spinster. It conjures up ghastly images of coldness, sadness and deprivation. (Bachelor is full of excitement and freedom.) The social taboo against being an autonomous woman is internalized. Self-containment and separateness feel selfish, self-centred, and even aggressive for a woman. They are out of the ordinary and somewhat frightening. Since connection to others must be maintained, a woman must make herself into a person others will find pleasing; in making herself in their image she may end up not knowing who she is. She loses herself.

The requirement of being connected to others and of deferring to them, in the ways we've discussed, leads to another psychological concomitant of woman's social role: that of having emotional antennae. A woman must learn to anticipate others' needs. The vulnerable and helpless infant who has no language needs a caretaker to read and intuit its unspoken messages and communications. A girl's life involves preparation for this skill and once acquired it is part of her psychology and something she brings to all relationships. The woman handles the emotional reins. This will be no less true in a work situation, where her emotional strengths will often be called upon. She must care for others and help them to express what they need, particularly at the emotional level. Once she has understood what others need, she must help them to satisfy those needs. Part of her social role as caretaker and nurturer of others involves putting her own needs second. Yet these needs do not remain merely secondary, they may often become hidden, for she does not have an emotional caretaker to turn to herself. There is an imbalance in the giving. A woman then carries deep feelings of neediness.

The intricacy of the psychosocial role of women is woven into the family in the relationships that will have most profound bearing on her psychological development. We turn now to the psychodynamics of woman's ego development to dissect the interactions that provide for the construction of a feminine psychology.

Drawing on the background that we have presented so far in human psychological development, gender identity and women's social position, we now explain our view of women's psychic structure and ego development. Ego development starts at birth and occurs within the context of the relationship that the infant has with its caretaker. Women's ego development is thus shaped in the mother–daughter relationship which is the critical relationship in the formation of women's psychology.

Mothers and daughters share a gender identity, a social role and social expectations. They are both second-class citizens within patriarchal culture and the family. In mothering a baby girl a woman is bringing her daughter up to be like her, to be a girl and then a woman. In mothering her son she is bringing him up to be other, to be a boy and then a man. Because of the social consequences of gender, mothers inevitably relate differently to their daughters and to their sons. Much of the difference is intentional and prescribed by the requirements of sex-role stereotyping (for example, encouraging an adolescent son's sexual adventures and restricting an adolescent daughter's sexual explorations); some of the difference is subtle and mothers may not be aware of it (girls are encouraged to be neat, messiness is tolerated in boys; or girls are encouraged to be 'pretty' and 'bright', boys to be 'bright'); and some of the differences of treatment come from a mother's unconscious feelings about being a woman and raising a daughter or raising a son.

In turning to the significance of the shared gender of mothers and daughters the first, most obvious, most important point is that all mothers were themselves and are themselves daughters. The second obvious and equally important point is that all daughters are brought up by their mothers to become mothers. The third point is that all mothers learned from their mothers about their place in the world. In each woman's experience is the memory – buried or active – of the struggles she had with her mother in the process of becoming a woman, of learning to curb her activities and to direct her interests in particular ways.

Mothers and daughters thus will have a tremendous amount of common experience, although this is often obscured by the fact that they are always in different phases of their social role vis-à-vis one another. Adult women with girl children play two roles simultaneously in the mother–daughter relationship: they are their mother's daughters and their daughter's mothers.

The interplay between a woman's conscious and unconscious feelings about being herself a daughter and a mother are an essential part of what she brings to maternal nurturance. The psychology of the mother that the infant girl will embody in the process of becoming a person will be imbued with mother's sense of self. Growing up female and being a woman means that one's sense of self reflects what each woman has had to learn in her development. The social requirements (of deference, submission and passivity) lead women to have many complicated feelings: often women do not feel complete, substantial or good in themselves; they feel afraid of their emotional needs, their insecurities and dependencies as well as fearful and guilty about their sexuality, their strivings for independence, nurturance and power.

The process of pregnancy, giving birth and becoming a mother can be a very satisfying experience. A new baby can be the fulfilment of an important personal desire, in which a woman's sense of self is enriched. Motherhood is the apex of woman's social role and in giving birth the woman receives approval from those around her. This valued aspect of her social role enables a woman to feel a certain contentment within herself. In turn she is able to transmit this positive sense of self to her daughter. Mother reads the communications of her daughter and is responsive. The infant in turn expresses her pleasure, and this communication adds to mother's feelings of self-worth and potency. Positive interactions between mother and daughter establish a pattern of relating and a feeling of closeness between the two of them. Mother gives to her daughter in this nurturing relationship the essential food for ego development which helps the infant establish its very sense of existence, security and well-being. The daughter's ego development is built on the feelings of acceptance and love in this most important first relationship.

Beyond these positive feelings that mother has towards herself, however, lie mother's other experiences of self. Deep inside each woman is a feeling that there is a part of her that is needy and uncared for, that she is undeserving, inadequate and inarticulate. She often feels that nobody sees her or gives her what she needs. She often feels that she cannot herself locate what she wants. These negative and complicated feelings she has about herself (consciously and unconsciously) have a profound effect on the daughter's psychology. Mother's negative self-image is as important a factor in the shaping of the mother–daughter interaction, and hence the daughter's psychology, as are her positive experiences of self.

We can identify the following major aspects of the mother–daughter interaction which make for a particular shaping of a daughter's psychology. The first of these is that the mother will *identify* with her daughter because of their shared gender, for when a woman gives birth to a daughter she is in a sense reproducing herself. When she looks at her daughter she sees herself.

> When my daughter was born each time I looked at her I thought she *was* me; I couldn't tell at all that she was different from me. You know that feeling when you look at yourself in a mirror, well it felt something like that. When my son was born that never even crossed my mind. He was different, he was something else (motioning 'out there' and 'away' with her hand). It was completely clear that he was a different person.

The daughter will follow in mother's footsteps. Mother must introduce her to the ways of behaving and feeling that go along with being a girl. She knows she must prepare her for a life spent, like hers, in taking care of others, attending to their needs, making a home and a baby, and for a place in society as a second-class citizen. When she looks at an infant son or at her little boy she sees someone who is quite other, who is going to have a very different life, and for whom she can imagine a whole world of differing possibilities. When she looks at her daughter she sees images of her own mothering, of her own experiences of childhood and growing up, of being a woman.

The second major aspect of the mother–daughter relationship is that a mother not only identifies with her daughter but also *projects* on to her some of the feelings she has about herself. She superimposes a part of herself – deeply buried feelings which are inaccessible and unconscious – and sees this part expressed in her daughter. In this projection she is seeing her daughter not as another person but as an extension of herself. Thus when she holds her infant daughter in her arms she reads the various communications of the child in a particular way. She sees a vulnerable, undefended, expressive, eager little girl. This in turn reawakens – still at an unconscious level – that part of her that feels needy, wanting to be nurtured, responded to and encouraged.

Mother in responding to her daughter is full of contradictory feelings, some of which she is aware of and some not. She wishes to respond to her daughter and meet her needs: sometimes she is able to and at other times she is not. The reasons are complex. On the one hand she hopes for a fuller and less restricted life for her daughter, while on the other she is fearful for a daughter who has not learned the essential feminine characteristics of restraining her own needs and desires and curbing her attempts towards independence. Of course, this is all unconscious: mother raises and relates to her daughter along the lines that she herself was raised. Unknownst to her she is caught in a paradox. Mother has the difficult task of showing her daughter how to limit her strivings towards independence. At the same time she must wean her very early on from relying, at an emotional level, upon having her dependency desires met. For mother to continue to meet them would go deeply against the grain of socialization to the feminine role. In other words mother cannot set up false expectations about what awaits a daughter in womanhood. Unconsciously mother gives the message to the daughter: 'Don't be emotionally dependent; don't expect the emotional care and attention you want; learn to stand on your own two feet emotionally. Don't expect too much independence; don't expect too much from a man; don't be too wild; don't expect a life too different from mine; learn to accommodate.' Mother demonstrates these unconscious injunctions by relating to her daughter in this way herself.

At the same time as mother pushes her daughter's neediness away she pulls her daughter to stay within the boundaries that she, herself, inhabits. Mother wishes to see contentment in her daughter, but she is again caught in a paradox for she herself does not have the experience of contentment. Mother has learned throughout her childhood to curb her desires and wants, to split her needs off, to hide that part of herself from others and not to expect to be responded to. Mother herself embodies a little girl inside herself, who has been hidden away.

This repressed little girl inside mother is a third important shaper of the mother–daughter relationship, for mother comes to be frightened by her daughter's free expression of her needs. Mother unconsciously acts towards her infant daughter in the same way as she acts internally to the little girl part of herself. The little daughter becomes an external representation of that part of herself which she has come to dislike and deny. The complex of feelings she feels as a result of her own deprivation through her childhood and her adult life is both directed inward in an internal struggle to negate the little girl part of herself and projected outward and transmitted to her daughter. Thus the developing girl comes to feel that both the needy and would-be independent parts of herself are wrong; that they must be hidden from her mother and the rest of the world.

These features of the mother–daughter interaction make for an extreme intensity in the relationship between the two of them. This intensity is marked by another feature – a staccato quality or an inconsistency in the relating. The inconsistency stems from the way a mother copes with her feeling of identification with her daughter and her own deep feelings about herself as a woman. At those times when mother relates to her daughter as a separate person she can be responsive and unambiguously caring. She can give her daughter what she needs, she can convey to her a sense of security and well-being. At other moments, however, mother's sense of herself as a separate person dissolves and she experiences her daughter and herself as having the same feelings, thoughts and desires [1]. When this occurs it is hard for a mother to be appropriately responsive; she is perhaps withdrawn at one instant and over-involved the next. She is acting on her unconscious feelings of identification and relating to her daughter in the same inconsistent way that she relates to the little girl part of herself. It is the toing and froing between a mother's sense of herself as separate and her merger with her daughter that combine to create the staccato quality of the relationship.

Although the nuances and particulars of each woman's experience vary, although what each woman brings to mothering is different, and although the specifics of each mother–daughter relationship are unique, these two crucial determinants – a mother's feelings about herself and her identification with her daughter – are reproduced in all mother–daughter relationships. They are the key features in the development of a woman's ego.

The shape of this relating, first established in infancy, continues throughout the daughter's life. As the daughter slowly becomes her own person and needs her mother in different ways, the intense, push–pull nature of the relationship persists. Through her relationship with mother the daughter is absorbing essential lessons about what it means to be female. Her mother is both model and guide and beyond that their relationship is absorbed by the daughter as a blueprint for other love relationships. The picture of mother that the daughter takes into herself is complex. Mother is the person who gives her what she needs – feeds her, bathes her, cuddles her, plays with her, talks to her, responds to her. She opens up wider and wider horizons. At the same time mother is the person who can say no, who can disappoint or withhold, who can be short-tempered and can misunderstand. Mother holds tremendous power – power to please and power to hurt. So many of mother's actions are incomprehensible. The daughter is the receiver of the contradictory messages in the push–pull dynamic. She experiences her mother giving the unconscious injunctions of staying close by but not expecting too much. The little girl cannot fathom why at times mother is so approving and loving and at other times so disappointed and disappointing. The little girl tries to make sense of mother's actions. The part of her that has felt nurtured and understood by mother, i.e. a psychological experience of solidity and goodness, has contributed to her ego development. But the daughter has also experienced that some parts of herself are not acceptable. The little girl absorbs the idea that in order to get love and approval she must show a particular side of herself. She must hide her emotional cravings, she must hide her disappointments and her angers, she must hide her fighting spirit, she must hide herself. She comes to feel that there must be something wrong with who she really is, which in turn must mean there is something wrong with what she needs and what she wants. A process of feeling inauthentic develops. She feels unsure in her reactions and distanced from her wants. This soon translates into feeling unworthy and hesitant about pursuing her impulses. Slowly she develops an acceptable self, one which appears self-sufficient and capable; one that is likely to receive more consistent acceptance. Here in this first relationship with mother the little girl learns to fear and hide away the little girl part of herself. She comes to feel like a fraud, for an external part of her is developing which is different from who she feels she is inside.

Meanwhile, at the psychic structural level a split occurs in the ego. This is not a conscious act but a protective feature of psychic structural development, for the hidden part (we call this the little-girl) has to go somewhere, it does not disappear. Because this part of her has not been responded to it has had to go underground and seek nurturance and acceptance within her inner world.

However, while this little-girl part of the ego still yearns for nurturance there is confusion about its rejection in the first place. Part of the ego tends to carry dreadful feelings, it is in isolation, depressed and despairing. When contact is possible she may be flooded with feelings of anger, disappointment or rejection. Hurt by the rejection, she may never want to show this needy part to anyone again. So her inner world constructs defences which protect this little-girl part of her from others and attempt to nourish and protect her internally. There is a whole world of relationships (internal object relations) which engage her. They both excite and disappoint the little-girl part. Mother continues to live on inside, alternately presenting herself as giver and withholder. She is still very powerful and still much needed. Inside, the little-girl is trying to challenge the deep conviction that if she shows herself she will continue to be rejected and disliked by those with whom she has relationships. In her private world she tries to rewrite history but time and again her previous painful experiences are reinforced. So the little-girl part builds boundaries; it is as though the needy, frightened part is surrounded by a fortress, a barrier. She cannot send messages out and others cannot penetrate her defences. Nobody can come in and hurt her and she cannot get out and hurt others or humiliate herself by exposing her needs.

The daughter hides the little-girl part of herself in this fortress because she has picked up a painful and powerful message from mother which tells her that she should not have expectations of being looked after emotionally, or of having her desires met, either by mother or by anyone else. Mother encourages her daughter to look to a man to be emotionally involved with. She teaches her daughter to direct her energies towards men and that she, as an adult, must come to depend on a man. But at the same time mother gives another message. As she lets her daughter know she must look to men, mother simultaneously transmits a message of disappointment and frustration. She conveys that *really* her daughter must not expect the man to come through for her or to understand her. Mothers often let their daughters know both overtly and covertly that men are disappointments. Mother conveys disdain and contempt for men. So what mother displays as the options for a daughter is tinged with ambivalence. She conveys both the possibilities and the impossibilities of a daughter's emotional ties to a man. Even though the daughter comes to look towards men she still yearns for mother's support and care. *From girlhood to womanhood women live with the experience of having lost these aspects of maternal nurturance. This nurturance is never replaced. Women look to men to mother them but remain bereft. These needs for nurturance do not decrease any the less for the loss. This loss, which causes tremendous pain, confusion, disappointment, rage and guilt for the daughter, is buried and denied in the culture at large as well as in the unconscious of the little girl.*

As we have discussed before, the infant who has had sufficient contact to embody its caretaker comes to feel secure within itself. The baby has a certain confidence that its needs will be met and that the larger world it can now see outside itself and mother is full of exciting possibilities, pleasures and new relationships. As the baby begins to separate from mother it feels its individuality and its differences. For the developing girl, still yearning for mother's reassurance, psychological separation and individuation can only be partial. The experience of the initial relating with mother means that the girl is left with feelings of deprivation, unworthiness and rejection. As she still needs mother very badly it is hard for her to feel unambiguously receptive to new experiences or to have confidence that others will be receptive to her needs and desires. She tries to move towards others to express herself but at the same moment she feels nervous, disloyal and abandoned. Attempts at separation take place under conditions of opposition and fear. There is no feeling of strength and wholeness which makes the world appear exciting; instead the world outside is tantalizing and frightening. In some ways it echoes aspects of the painful inner world of the child's reality. Mother is still a focal point; she encourages some attempts at separation – indeed pushes them – and thwarts others. Because the little-girl part of the girl's ego structure has been split off, it continues to be deprived of the nourishment and contact that it needs for maturation. The girl both fears and longs to remerge with mother and to be held and cared for. But the inconsistency in the relating pushes her towards separation, with the construction of boundaries between herself and the little-girl inside. These are in some sense false boundaries; they do not come from an integrated ego structure which can clearly distinguish between her and the outside world, rather they are internal boundaries, separating one part of herself from another part and keeping the little-girl inside shut away from the outside world. At the same time, the daughter's sense of self is fused with her sense of mother. In her attempts to separate from mother she may not know who she is. In trying to be her own person she is confused as to where she begins and mother ends. Through her early development she has taken mother into her and because she does not have a strong sense of her own separate self, the sense of mother inside her may outweigh her own independent identity. Unlike her brother, she cannot use gender difference to differentiate herself from mother. She is a mini-version of mother, someone who will have a life like mother's.

And so her sense of self as unique, separate and other is entwined with a sense of mother. There is a shared social role, a shared prescription for life, a shared psychology.

The daughter's attempts at separation are then somewhat ambiguous and dovetail with mother's ambivalence. For although the message from mother during the period of infantile dependency has been, 'Take care of yourself, don't depend on others, don't want too much,' these injunctions, which in effect seem to push the daughter away, combine with another unstated, unconscious message which is, 'Stay close, don't stray, don't go too far, it's dangerous.' In other words the process towards separation includes a tug to stay close to mother and to share the boundaries that she inhabits. As daughter tries to separate from mother, mother in turn must let go just enough. She must allow her daughter to explore the limits of her new identity from a safe and secure base. This giving out and setting of boundaries that the daughter and mother negotiate requires enormous emotional and psychological shifting for the mother. Very early on the mother may experience a tension between her daughter's utter dependence and helplessness on her which confirms her essentiality and her desires for the child's separateness. The mother may be both reassured by being needed as she simultaneously resents and begrudges her own loss of independence.

Mother's wish to keep her daughter close reflects in turn her own psychology and social experience. If mother has been living through her child, has accrued her identity through her mothering, then she may have great difficulty in letting her daughter separate. She may need to keep her daughter close to her in order to maintain this sense of herself. A daughter's moves towards independence do diminish mother's sense of being needed and her sense of who she is may be endangered. Because the woman has been brought up to see her central role as mother, she may feel empty, depressed and confused about who she is, and may lose a sense of purpose when her child separates. With the period of separation–individuation the mother may already feel that she is 'losing' her child, in a foretaste of future separations (nursery, school, adolescence) that jolts and hurts. With a daughter, mother clings on to the hope that she can live her life through her daughter's future experiences, that her daughter will not abandon her.

Because mother's psychological development has been similar to her daughter's, and mother herself has not had a solid experience of selfhood, of separation, she too has false boundaries. Her daughter's moving away involves a loss at the psychic structural level as mother has attempted to complete herself in her attachment and merger with her daughter. Mother's merger with her daughter blurs the distinction between the two of them.

As mother now pulls her daughter to stay close, as she indicates to her the shape of a girl's life, she instructs her in an essential feminine skill. She teaches her to look after others. The daughter, in hiding her little-girl part, becomes extremely sensitive to neediness in others. She develops antennae that pick up the needs of others; *she learns to give what others need; she starts to give to others out of the well of her own unmet needs*.

As the mother transmits to her daughter the importance of caring for others she brings to the relationship her *own* unmet emotional needs. Inside each mother lives a hungry, needy, deprived and angry little-girl. She turns to her daughter for nurturance. She looks to her to make up the loss of her own maternal nurturance and to satisfy her continued yearnings. The psychological attachment and lack of separation between mothers and daughters and daughters and mothers exists through generations of women. The daughter becomes involved in a cycle that is part of each woman's experience, attempting to care for mother. As the daughter learns her role as nurturer, *her first child is her mother*.

As the daughter grows up she looks at all the women around her – her mother, grandmother, aunts, teachers, sisters, film stars, images in storybooks and magazines – and consciously and subconsciously takes in and tries to form a future image of herself as a woman. She looks to them as she develops her own sexuality. How she manages her sexuality will be very important for it is through this aspect of herself that she will find her place in the world.

Woman everywhere is viewed in her relationship to her sexuality. Feminist commentators have drawn attention to the dichotomous ways in which women are seen and experience themselves and their sexuality. One side of the dichotomy is the image of the virgin princess, the longing to be possessed as yet untouched father's daughter, father's possession. The woman is pure, naïve, expectant and adoring; she will give herself to the right man, but her body is more spiritual than carnal. On the other side of the dichotomy is the image of the woman who is actively sexual, perhaps bewitching, Mata Hari or the whore, ravenous and rapacious and very exciting. The woman who stands outside of the family, the single woman, the woman who is not attached within a sexual relationship, represents women's unharnessed sexuality. She carries an aura which both men and women respond to with awe and fear; she represents a threat to the given order.

But whichever side of the dichotomy the woman pursues in an expression of her womanhood, or if she attempts to straddle both images, her sexuality is always formed with an idea of the image she can create. For female sexuality is not simply experienced by the woman as an aspect of herself that she can enjoy and communicate; it is, because of her social position, both a product for herself and her product in the world. Women's sexuality has been a means by which women have found their place, whatever their social class and ethnic background. The paradoxical position of female sexuality being the vehicle for a woman finding a home, so to speak, and yet having once found it needing to hide her sexuality or channel it into producing babies, means that all women live with the split of having to be simultaneously sexual and yet having to curb their sexuality.

However, it is a misnomer to talk of sexuality as a thing, a separate entity. Sexuality is another thread of human contact. It is a physical, erotic, energetic experience; a communication, a contact with another. Just as emotional love and caring has its own language without words, so too is sexuality a language, a unique human intimate experience. This potential connection is constructed and channelled along specific paths according to the laws of a given culture. Masculinity and femininity are constructed in particular ways in patriarchal culture, similarly female and male sexuality have their particular form in contemporary society.

Viewing sexuality this way we can see that female sexuality is an aspect of self that like other aspects develops in and is brought to relationships. The mother–daughter relationship contains a sexual component itself at the same time as it is a prelude for a girl's future sexual relations. In this sense, then, the mother-daughter relationship provides an initial shaping of a daughter's sexuality.

Mothers both relate physically and erotically to their young daughters at the same time as they hold back, cut off or contain that aspect of relating in the relationship.

In our practice we have heard mothers express difficulty with the erotic feelings they have towards their babies. Often the experience of sexual connection is cut short and restrained. For the infant this is like a broken circuit, like the push–pull dynamic. In a parallel sense to mother's curbing her little-girl inside, so too she has come to manage her sexuality. Just as she transmits so many messages to her daughter about who she will be as a woman, so too does mother transmit what her daughter's sexuality can be.

The mother's feelings about her own body and her sexuality are critical, how a mother feels about her body influences strongly how a daughter will come to feel about her own body. Nancy Friday writes:

> When we were learning to walk, mother helped us practice and her confidence in our success encouraged us to keep trying. When it came to sex her emotions became communicated to us too, this time what we learned from her was anxiety and failure. [2]

The complex cultural attitudes towards women's bodies – that they are sexual, ugly, mysterious, extraordinary, dark, bloody and smelly – find a place in each woman's sense of her self. The female body is both degraded and deified; it is so powerful that men will dissipate themselves or die for it. The female body and female sexuality are held responsible for male sexuality and male aggression (with, as an extreme example, the myth that it is a woman's fault if a man rapes her). Women, then, come to their relationship with their daughters with, at the very least, apprehension about the female body and the power of female sexuality.

In this context, adolescence can be a terribly difficult and confusing time for a girl. It is a critical period in the development of her sexuality. A girl's body is changing in many ways, sometimes quite dramatically over a very short period of time. All of the ideas the girl has about women, her mother and sex, are facing her at once and feel somewhat out of her control. Information that she has been given about these changes, her forthcoming period, her developing breasts and her sexual feelings have an importance in how she comes to feel about herself and her sexuality. Because of mother's complicated relation to her own sexuality it is often impossible for her to transmit the potential richness of what is happening to her daughter. Many girls may first hear about periods, developing breasts and pubic hair from girl-friends and magazines, or their mothers may tell them the facts and leave it at that. In most cases these things are talked about in whispers or privately and rarely with the father. There is a lot of shame and embarrassment about what is happening to the girl's body. In our practice we hear time and time again about the ways in which sexuality was either totally hidden or not spoken of in the family; a hint of sexuality could produce an electric edge of embarrassment. Rarely do we hear a woman tell us that sexuality was openly accepted, that the parents' sexuality was visible, that mother or father had informed the girl of the changes her body would go through in a positive and exciting way, that her body would become a woman's body and that would be a joyful proud transition. We hear instead remembrances of shame, embarrassment, fear, of not liking breasts because they were too big or too small, of not liking pubic hair, large hips and rounded bottoms. Added to this women recall adolescent warnings of caution and restriction. Female sexuality seems to be dangerous; it is unknown, unspoken. You must have 'it' in order to become a grown-up woman and yet you must hide 'it'. So many adolescent girls and young women learn to be frightened of their own sexuality and to dislike their own bodies. Many daughters see their mothers as non-sexual and know that they do not want to be like her in that respect.

From quite an early age she may be aware of not wanting to be like her mother – she wants to be a different sort of woman. She may want to be 'sexy' like the film star or the lady at the hairdressers – unlike her mother. She may feel ashamed of the way her mother dresses or embarrassed by her behaviour. Whether mother conveys her sexuality through dress, physicality, etc. or hides it, it will make an impression on her daughter. The daughter may be comparing herself and her sexuality to her mother as she tries to find her own independent sexuality.

So adolescence heralds the convergence of new events as the young woman's sexuality explodes. It drives her to seek freedom and independence from her family simultaneously. Her new sexual body means that she comes face to face with both her reproductive and her erotic capacities.

41

This is a painful time for a girl for she already experiences a tremendous discomfort about her sexuality, and knows that women's social heritage does not allow her to act on her new desires for freedom.

The thread of sexuality is entwined in the issues of separation and merger for women, although its meaning will not always be confluent. Sexual connection with another unveils woman's attempt to separate from mother. But sexuality is contained within marriage and the family. Her physical attachment with another symbolizes her relatedness outside the family, but this new relatedness highlights the complexities of separation and attachment for women. Cultural law dictates that the only way a woman can leave her family is by moving to start another family. She leaves her parents' home to go to her husband's. There is no place in the world for her as an independent, separate, sexual woman. In patriarchy the daughter is passed from father to husband – as ritualized in the wedding ceremony, where the bride is 'given away' by the father. But it is the mother who is crying near by, filled with the sense of loss of her daughter. The paradox lies in the fruition of mother's ambiguous message. On the one hand, mother has instructed her daughter to go towards a man; on the other, this eventuality brings mother tremendous pain, for she experiences the loss of her daughter. (Mother's own memory of leaving her mother may also be unconsciously re-evoked.) The marriage highlights the cultural prohibition of the impossibility of separation – psychological and social – for women. She must leave home and yet she cannot. Women are at psychic crossroads.

The psychic crossroad of marriage and sexuality brings into focus another aspect of woman's ego development. The non-separated nature of women's ego may mean that for a woman sexual connection with a partner brings with it a fear of loss of self. During sexual activity a woman is experiencing the prominence of the sensual and erotic thread in human connection. Her sexuality flows through her body and connects with another. Other forms of communication such as language, conscious thinking processes and discourse move into the background. This deeply gratifying sensual communication is an adult ideal. But because of women's (and men's) false boundaries (men's false boundaries arise from their defensive separation from mother at separation–individuation), this form of communication is often problematic. The woman, unsure of her boundaries, may feel unable to get out of her head, into her body and allow herself to let go. Or she may feel taken over in the sexual merger with a lover. In order to have a pleasurable and satisfying sexual experience one must be able to let go. In order to merge with another one must have a defined sense of self to return to. Because adult sexuality echoes aspects of mother–infant pre-verbal sensuality in its very unique communication, sexuality and merger may stir up deeply resonant early physical experience before there was a definite sense of self and before language.

Because of the psychic non-separation from mother and because of mother's injunctions about female sexuality – and daughter's sexuality – a woman may find that her attachment to mother is expressed in unwittingly 'taking her to the bedroom'. The daughter feels guilt in her attempts to connect with another, unconsciously she feels she has abandoned mother. In addition, she has internalized that sex is shameful. In this sense, then, a female sexuality is shaped in the mother–daughter relationship, which in turn is folded into culture. Female sexuality is experienced as shameful and problematic. A woman's sexuality develops within another constraint, that is, the overwhelming cultural pressures towards heterosexuality.

Women never experience a free choice of sexual partners. TV screens and newspapers bombard the young woman with pictures of monogamous heterosexual life. Most families are organized on monogamous hetero-sexual lines and the young woman is guided by parents and teachers towards the correct ways of relating to other young women and young men. Sexual experiences with other girls are thus furtive and often cast in heterosexual terms. The overwhelming actuality and image of heterosexuality means that by adolescence young women attracted to other young women feel that there is something wrong. Despite these pressures, many girls do have sexual experiences with other girls and may continue to have sexual rela-tionships with women throughout their adult life. More often than not, however, because of social pressures many women turn to men for their sexual life.

The construction of a feminine psychology and sexuality occurs mainly within the mother–daughter relationship. It is a psychology and sexuality which fits in with the social requirements of a patriarchal order. A girl is brought up to a life directed towards caring for others. Her own unmet needs provide a basis from which she gives. A girl is brought up with the idea that she always must be connected to others. Her shaky boundaries and her yearnings for maternal nurturance mean that she is always striving to be close to others who can help fill the gap and make her feel whole. A girl is brought up to put her needs second; her feelings of unworthiness ensure that she will have a sense of herself which is imbued with a certain insecurity. Her sense of safety within herself is ambiguous and her ego development combines a split-off part that contains the needy little-girl and the defences against the needs. These features of a woman's psychology are a refraction at the psychic level of her social position. Her ego structure reflects this.

The daughter's personality takes shape in her relationship with her mother, a relationship weighed heavy with longing, identification, disappointment, betrayal, anger and guilt. As mothers transmit the knowledge of how to survive within the structure that they and all women inhabit, they bind their daughters with the chains of femininity.

The entwining of a daughter's life with that of her mother means they share complex and powerful emotions of love, neediness, insecurity, low self-esteem and identification. Many women never feel free of their mothers. They are not separate people, but experienced as mother living inside, judging, binding, tempting and disappointing. At the same time mothers and daughters often feel the pain of not being able to share honestly, to expose in direct ways, who they are.

As Adrienne Rich writes: 'Mother stands for the victim in ourselves, the unfree woman, the martyr. Our personalities seem dangerously to blur and overlap with our mothers.' The consequence of this painful identification is that we deny that our mother has anything to do with us: 'We develop matraphobia and try to split ourselves off from her, to purge ourselves of her bondage, in a desperate attempt to know where mother ends and daughter begins, we perform radical surgery' [3].

The Father–Daughter Relationship

While father is a very important person in the girl's world, he rarely is the centre of it during the first two years of her life. In fact father is strikingly absent. Time with father may consist of an hour at night, five minutes in the morning. Under these circumstances time with father may be experienced as pleasurable, exciting or perhaps a little frightening. Father may be adored or feared or somewhere in between. But however he is experienced by the daughter, he is special, he does not inhabit the girl's world on a regular basis, he is exotic. Perhaps important for all girls' psychological development is the fact that *father is constantly leaving*; he does not stay and share in the girl's world with her mother. A girl grows up with a preconscious knowledge of the limited time and contact she will have with a man.

In a little girl's early life father is someone outside the relationship and the world she inhabits with mother. When he enters their orbit the nuances of the primary communication change, for he represents and is in his presence someone from outside. He brings with him his experience and an aura of the world outside the home; he symbolizes maleness, worldliness and separateness. (Siblings, who are outside the primary orbit, are nevertheless part of the world of home.)

The little girl learns that father is very important to family survival, and that his daily abandonment is for the purpose of providing security – economic security – for the family. Daughter learns that he is the one on whom she must learn to rely. She sees the complexity of mother's relationship with father. She sees that father depends on mother for many things. His daily life is an expression of his need for a woman in order to survive. His dependency needs are met in an unstated way at home, emotionally and physically.

The girl may feel excluded and pushed away from mother when father is around. She may feel she does not have the power to hold mother in the same way. She may feel jealous of mother's availability to another. And she may feel excluded from her parents' relationship. The little girl comes to learn that her parents are a couple. From her infancy, she and mother were a couple; as she develops, her awareness of the world shifts and she is confronted by mother and father as a couple. She takes in how important a man is in a woman's life. The little girl sees that mother has a partner. Whether or not the marriage is satisfactory and cooperative the little girl sees the intensity of her parents' relationship. The seeds for her own future relating to a man are fertilized. She watches mother and follows her. She learns to relate to father in specific ways. She learns that an important part of their relationship is pleasing him. She is encouraged to transfer her primary dependency from her mother to her father – the embodiment of all future males; she must learn to become a woman in heterosexual society. (As we have discussed, mother's relationship with daughter is shaped by this requirement and is expressed in the push–pull dynamic.)

The daughter is encouraged to depend on her father in the following ways: he is the link to the world outside the family and the daughter must use him as access to that world. He is more secure and sure of himself in the world and so she can imagine that he will protect her. However, she cannot identify with father, because of his sexual identity. Father has encouraged his daughter to charm him and a male audience, to attract and hold his attention in specifically defined feminine ways, as she will later need to do. She learns that she must not attempt to make decisions which challenge his authority, to show too much independence and power.

Very few little girls have much contact with their fathers in the critical period of ego development. Father does play a tremendously important role, but he builds on the ego development that occurs between mother and daughter. Father is another person with whom the daughter can identify when she is in the process of separation–individuation. As she tries to differentiate herself from her mother by being different, the girl may look to father and try to emulate him. Aspects of father's personality can often be seen in a daughter. She may try to incorporate the characteristics of him that she admires: outgoing, humorous, storytelling etc.

The various facets of father's relationship with his daughter are complex. He stands outside of the physical experience of pregnancy, birth and lactation. He may feel excluded from the mother–child relationship. He may feel inadequate to meet it. He may really appreciate the sensuality and tenderness that it brings him in his life, and he may feel that he very much wants to participate in it as fully as he can, but he will be somewhat tentative about his place. Because of his lack of preparedness for 'mothering' he may feel inadequate in relating to the baby (this, of course, may be unconscious). His own insecurities and lack of experience may be met by mother's anxiety about a father's capabilities at mothering. In her worry about his inexperience mother may unintentionally undercut his confidence. His feelings about having a daughter or having a son will inevitably influence his relationship to a new baby. With a daughter, particularly, he may feel in the dark about who she is, what to do with her, how to relate. With a boy child he can rely on his own experience of boyhood and maleness to aid him in his relationship.

In the early mother–infant couple father may feel excluded and jealous. His relationship with his partner has changed with the entry of the third person. His partner is no longer available to him in the same way. If the child is a girl his feeling of exclusion and/or being the 'outsider' in the triangle may be increased. At the same time the closeness between mother and infant may re-evoke his own experience of infancy, when he was very close to a woman.

In our practice many women report having no real contact with their fathers. They wonder where father fits in their lives. We often find that a daughter's relationship with father was not straightforward, that she experienced barriers and interceptions. Mother lives in the father–daughter relationship. Father's relating lovingly to his daughter may cause friction, because mother may experience both jealousy at his attention to daughter as well as anger because of what she feels is lacking in her life. Mother may feel that father shows gentle, caring affection to a daughter in ways that he cannot with her. Mother's needy little girl inside yearns for just this type of attention and so seeing it between her partner and their daughter can be painful. Mothers may unwittingly intercept this loving contact between a father and a daughter.

In addition, because father spends so little time each day with a daughter, unlike mother, his availability to his daughter in those moments may stir up resentment in mother. Mother sees her daughter thrilled by the adoration of father and perhaps feels the negation of all she gives.

These dynamics in the mother–father–daughter triangle are all a part of the girl's psychological development. The daughter's relationship to father is undeveloped. Because she is so attached to her mother and because her antennae are so finely developed, the daughter picks up mother's ambivalent feelings about daughter's relationship to father. The daughter may have to hide the contact she does have with him or feel guilty about it. Another dynamic we have consistently seen in our practice is that of a daughter's alliance with mother about father's inadequacies. Women often express contempt and disdain for their fathers. The daughter finds herself involved in mother's anger towards father. Indeed often it is the daughter who carries mother's rage. Women report feeling their fathers to be weak because they did not 'stand up' to mother. 'He wasn't strong enough to stop mother's interceptions.' 'He didn't fight for a relationship with his daughter.' Once again daughter and mother share an experience. They both feel disappointed in relation to father. They both feel anger and disdain. Mothers and daughters thus tighten their unspoken bond in disappointment. Father's position in the emotional triangle of the family is a critical piece in women's difficulty in psychological separation. For neither does the father–daughter relationship provide for unambiguous relating. Father is outside daughter's primary ambivalent relationship with mother but he cannot offer an unambivalent one himself.

This ambivalence in the father's relating continues through to adolescence. As the girl becomes a woman father may withdraw physically while at the same time becoming more protective towards the daughter, transmitting to her fear and danger signals about boys, being grown up, and leaving home. The father–daughter relationship illustrates one of the tragedies of patriarchy. A man's position in the family and the significance of gender in his early psychological development means that men are both ill prepared to give nurturance and at the same time scared of women [4]. Men do not provide the emotional stability for girls and women to turn to either in girl's early struggles for psychological separation or in adult heterosexual relationships.

Father, then, stands at once outside the mother–daughter relationship and is the representative of the patriarchal order. Symbolically he represents many things for the girl which are different from the world of women, from the world of her mother, the world she is supposed to enter into.

In the daughter's psychology and ego development we can dissect the ensemble of social relations that exist and are reproduced in the patriarchal nuclear family.

III The Feminist Psychotherapy Relationship: The Beginning and Middle Stages

Psychoanalysis and psychotherapy originally developed in the nineteenth century as a treatment for mental distress to help the individual who was suffering to experience herself or himself as living more fully in the world and less bounded by emotional distress such as anxiety, depression, or hysterical symptoms. The practice of a psychoanalytically oriented feminist therapy is also concerned with trying to relieve the distressing symptoms that prevent a woman from feeling comfortable with and within herself. However, in our examination into the underlying causes of distress, we see the relationship between the intensely private, internal world – the psychic reality of the individual woman – and the external world, a patriarchal world which shapes her and within which she lives and develops. In our therapy we try to illuminate this internal world and reveal its profound influence on aspects of the woman's daily life. The therapy relationship provides the means to explore the structure of the woman's individual psyche, the workings of her unconscious, and, of course, it facilitates the change that is desired and agreed upon.

Much of the psychological development theory we will be discussing has come out of our observations of particular aspects of the therapy relationship itself – and this is how psychoanalytic theory has always been constructed, from practice to theory. The process of psychotherapy centres on two features: one is the actual content, what therapists call the material that the client discusses with the therapist, for example problems within relationships, problems within oneself, problems with work, anxieties, fantasies, specific symptoms. The second feature is the relationship between the two different people engaged in psychotherapy together, the client and the therapist. In classical psychoanalysis the view is held that there is a transference relationship and a reality relationship between the client and the therapist [1]. Transference is not a very complicated concept and is a common occurrence in everyday life. It is the phenomenon of bringing one's emotional responses from the past, the ones that we have acquired from childhood, into everyday life. We bring who we are into all rela-

48

tionships and transference means that we are assigning, i.e. transferring, feelings, attitudes and behaviours which make up who we were, but also the feelings and behaviours and attitudes that we now have towards other people that originated in our relations to others from infancy. While transference occurs frequently in everyday life these transference manifestations are cut short by the actual responses of others with whom one relates, who do not fit into one's internal scheme, who do not take on the transference feelings. Thus new relationships can challenge deeply held emotional pictures, as people seek to change their experience. Equally, new relationships can repeat old patterns and thereby confirm old ways of relating. The psychotherapeutic situation provides a place for the study and examination of the origin and persistence of transference feelings that may arise in the client in relation to the therapist. (Freud's observations of the transference relationship provided him with the data to build his theory about psychological development.)

Classical psychoanalysts saw transference as originating in the repetition compulsion, where the person continually re-enacts a form of behaviour as a way to come to grips with it. Transference feelings belong to significant figures, usually parents, from the past, which are now displaced and projected on to the person of the therapist. In this light transference to the analyst was inevitably understood in libidinal terms, with the analyst representing the longed-for Oedipal parent. Modern developments in psychodynamic therapy have shifted from interpreting the transference relationship as an expression of the irresolution of the Oedipus complex to a much earlier developmental stage from which the individual brings to therapy a distilled picture of her or his very early relationships to others (that is, her or his internal object relations). (See Appendix for developments from psychoanalysis to psychodynamic therapy, and references to Oedipus complex.) For many modern theorists it is this pre-Oedipal period that is crucial in the formation of psychic structure. In therapy and within the transference relationship the therapist will be working towards an understanding of the client's experience of the external world in terms of her or his object relations.

A feminist view of transference can incorporate both these views, the classical and modern. We draw on the information we gather from what is happening between the therapist and the person in therapy to build up our psychological development theory of little girls and of women. From our perspective the most critical relationship that is going to come up in the transference is that between mother and daughter. Uncovering the dynamics of the mother–daughter relationship within the therapy provides an understanding of the steps of feminine personality development.

49

There is a real relationship between the two people doing therapy together which in our work is central to the reparative work. The two women [2] in the room are relating to each other, and although there will be resonances of past relationships that will be worked on and utilized in the therapy, there is also a new and real relationship beginning between them.

The Beginning Stage of Therapy

Let us look closely at the beginning of the therapy relationship, when a woman client and a woman therapist meet for the first time. For the client this is a big step and an extremely sensitive time. She has been able to admit to herself and another that she needs help, although at this point she may not be able to put into words what her problems are. The client brings her distress, her need and desire to be helped, together with her fear, nervousness and anxiety, and tries to explain to her therapist what her problem (often called the 'presenting problem') is.

The therapist has three tasks at this stage. First, she must be able to empathize with the initial concerns of the client, and by her manner convey this to the client. For many women feel extremely vulnerable entering therapy, especially if it is the first time, and many feel very unsure of what to do and how to do it. It is the therapist's responsibility to provide a certain shaping and boundaries so that the woman can gradually come to feel safe. Second, she has to provide the client with information about the therapy, such as the fees, time of appointments, etc. She may need to explain a bit about the process of therapy. The therapist needs to talk about her theoretical biases [3] so that the client knows what kind of therapy she is committing herself to. Where possible the therapist will also need to discuss with the client treatment goals and methods, since, for example, it is most disconcerting for a woman to enter therapy with anxiety about a specific presenting problem such as a phobia only to discover months later that the therapist's view of a useful treatment model is to remove the emphasis from direct discussion of the phobia. Third, throughout the first months of therapy, the therapist must work hard to provide a context within which the client can open up to her. She must listen very carefully to what her client is saying on several levels. She is trying to understand what the client's experience is, to feel what the client is feeling. A therapist may come out of a session with strong feelings which, when analysed, she can see have been transmitted to her by the client.

For example, a therapist may feel quite sad after a session and she needs to think about her sadness in relation to what her client was sharing with her. (The therapist must of course sort out first whether this is identification or countertransference.) The client during the session was telling of something sad but expressing this with no affect, in quite an unemotional way so that the therapist ended up feeling and carrying the sadness. What the therapist feels after a session is very useful in the beginning stages of therapy; it is a communication from the client.

In the beginning stages of therapy the client will probably be talking about a particular situation that she has just experienced, or is currently experiencing, in her life. The therapist is trying to listen and help the client to understand what that experience means for her. She is giving to her client in an immediate way by showing her concern and trying to clarify with the client what she is actually saying and experiencing. In this way the client feels less isolated in her pain and the experience of being understood is starting. For in our therapy we make an assumption that the woman has not felt herself to be accurately heard or understood, that she has not before had the opportunity to describe in detail the complexities of her psychological experience. An essential part of the therapy lies in building a relationship in which the client can have a reasonable expectation of being heard and understood. The interventions, be they questions or interpretations, by the therapist are part of the process by which the therapist is indicating her willingness to be available and accepting.

At the same time, the therapist is absorbing information about the psychology of the client. She is drawing out the underlying issues, the underlying psychology of the woman, in order to be able to work with and help her client. The client is talking about a particular situation and the therapist is trying to help with that situation, but at the same time she is using its wider ramifications and implications to build up a picture of the psychology of the particular woman. In these early meetings the therapist is sketching a developmental picture – a picture of the woman's internal object relations.

The therapist is experiencing the client in this new relationship. She is alert to how the client actually presents herself, how she sits, how she communicates her emotions, where there are obvious blocks, how she is affecting the therapist, ways in which she comes into the room, ways in which she keeps or misses her appointments, whether she comes to her sessions on time, early, late. The therapist is also taking in what happens at the beginning of the session – the quality, the texture, the feeling of the client, and how that may change over the course of the session – and what happens at the end of the session, in the last ten minutes, how the client leaves the therapist. All these important details will contribute to the larger picture that will be developed over the course of the therapy, about who the client is and what the therapy relationship will be.

Above all, in this early stage of therapy, the therapist is trying to begin to build a sense of trust. The client is sitting on the other side of the room and it is the therapist's job to enable a bridge to be built between them. The therapist reaches out to the client to help her to make contact.

Many clients do not know what is supposed to happen in therapy. In these early sessions it is important for the therapist to give some reassuring information about the process of therapy. For example, that it is a relationship between the two people in the room: that it will take time for the therapist to understand the client but that is what she wants to do and is what she is there for. The therapist also needs to provide the client with new ways of looking at her experience and at who she is, and to reassure her. that the ways of being and coping she has used in the past can be rejected if they are no longer helpful. What the therapist is providing for her client is the possibility of change. At this stage the therapist is perhaps the potential lifeline or anchor for the client. We say potential lifeline because what is happening in the beginning stages of therapy is that the client is protecting herself: she is cautious, she is taking stock of her therapist. She is not necessarily making an immediate link with her. She has hopes and expectations but she is also asking herself, 'Will this person actually be able to help me, will this person actually be able to understand who I am, can I be helped, is it all hopeless, dare I open myself up to this person, dare I bring my needs into this relationship, am I going to be disappointed?' (the thoughts are conscious and unconscious).

These protections that the client brings into the relationship with her are called defences. Defences are seen to be psychological protective mechanisms with which people defend and protect themselves against painful interaction, against painful feelings. The aim in psychoanalysis is to interpret the defences and thereby get through to the feelings and the fears and the developmental block in which the person is trapped.

One view within psychoanalytic practice is that from the very beginning the therapist should interpret the client's defences and analyse them for the client. Interpretation of defences takes place in two ways; the therapist can interpret defences that a client has outside therapy – for example in a situation with a friend or a lover; or the therapist can interpret the defences that the client brings into the therapy relationship. Different schools of psychoanalysis have specific ways of interpreting defences.

(In some schools an interpretation of a defence can sound like an attack. We do not share this approach. For example, a client meets a therapist for the first time; the therapist knows nothing of the client and the client knows nothing of the therapist. The analyst believes the client should come for psychoanalysis or psychotherapy at least three times a week. The client, who knows very little about therapy at this point says, 'Well, actually I was thinking more of coming once a week to therapy; I thought that's what therapy was about,' and maybe, 'That's all that I can afford,' as well. The therapist interprets the client's wanting to come to therapy only once a week as a defence and says, 'I think that you may be afraid of letting yourself open up to me. You don't want to help yourself, you're not letting yourself get well.' This example shows how something can be interpreted as a defence which we may not see as a defence at all, because the client may just not know of the unwritten 'rules' about how often to come to therapy. If in fact we did believe that therapy three times a week was very important we would discuss with the client why we thought so and have a dialogue about what the client felt about coming to therapy once, twice or three times a week. The important thing would be for the client to have the choice. The client is half the therapy relationship and we would respect her power and her impact within the relationship throughout the therapy, and especially at the beginning. For instance, continuing with the example, we might say, 'Well, why don't we start once a week and see how it goes, and discuss coming more times a week as we go along.' If coming once a week was indeed some sort of protection or defence, we would store this information about the client and share it with her at a later date if it reflected other aspects of her personality and could be useful to her.)

Precisely because the client comes into the therapy room feeling vulnerable we think it important that her vulnerability is not further exposed until she feels helpless. We must confirm that she can be self-determining within the therapy situation and that the two of us can work out together what actually is important for her.

We see defences as operating on two levels. Defences may indeed act against the interests of the client; they may be psychological mechanisms which push people away, keep people at a distance and even aid in the promotion of bad relationships. But on the other hand defences have been constructed as a protection for the client; they came from difficult dynamics in central relationships in the first place and developed as a result of hurt, rejection, loss, pain and anger. In one sense, too, defences are creative mechanisms of human beings to protect themselves in the world.

We think it is important to acknowledge both aspects of a particular defence. In our experience any sort of attack or criticism of the defence strengthens it, makes the client feel frightened and also feel that something is going to be taken away from her, something which she still needs. In our practice we have found that it is only through the therapist's acceptance of the defences as a part of the therapy relationship that progress will be made. The therapist in a sense has to peek behind the defence to see what the client may be trying to express. She does not get put off by the defences. She provides the sense that the relationship is a safe place for the client so that what the defences are protecting can slowly emerge. This acceptance of the defences by the therapist enables the two people slowly to come to look at and recognize the defences together. References to the defences become part of the language that therapist and client share. Only when the client feels trust, safety and security within the therapy relationship will the defences dissolve. In this beginning stage of therapy one might share this process with the client. The therapist indicates that in the process of the client feeling held, met and understood in the relationship, the defences will dissolve as the client finds new ways of being herself.

So from our theory of the psychic structural development of women, the defences we encounter in the therapy relationship can be understood in the following ways.

In women the defences are protecting the little girl inside, hidden away from the world. As we have seen, the woman may feel that her little girl is dangerous, unlovable; that the little girl will be rejected, as will her needs. So here the defences are operating on two levels. First, they are protecting the little girl inside from being hurt and rejected by others – this is what the woman is anticipating; second, the defences are protecting the person by whom the woman wants and needs to be cared for from that little girl inside, because the woman feels that this part of herself may be ugly, unlovable and violent and may push away or destroy her loved one.

A woman in therapy needs to expose her little-girl inside to the therapist, although she will not be aware of this at this stage of the therapy. She needs to be nurtured by her therapist, she needs to have a different experience with this new woman, but unconsciously this very part of herself is scared that the interaction will not be successful, that she will be rejected once again. And so the defences may be working to present an image to the therapist of a woman who does not have many needs, who does not have a little girl inside, who will not overburden the therapist.

So the little girl inside the woman comes into the therapy room with her defences and protections against her dependency desires, both these that she feels now and those that she has felt throughout her life. These intense feelings may emerge completely, albeit with enormous hesitancy. The woman may feel tremendous guilt and shame about her dependency desires and try to push them away. Even if she cannot articulate these desires, she inevitably feels that it is inappropriate to have these needs and to want them understood and satisfied by the therapist. This may well be happening at a subliminal level. In the beginning stages of therapy the therapist must reassure the client that it is acceptable to express the dependency desires and encourage her to explore her wishes. Together they can help relieve the client of the guilt that imprisons these feelings.

The freeing of these feelings, the exploration of them, their meaning and their satisfaction, are a major focus in the middle and most prolonged stage of the therapy relationship.

The Middle Stage

The middle stage of therapy lasts anywhere from six months to five or six years. By now a relationship between client and therapist has been established. There is a basis of trust. The therapist has provided concrete help for the client in dealing with different aspects of her life and understanding herself better in all kinds of situations. Together they have built a shared language and understanding – a way of looking at and expressing what is happening in the client's internal world.

A central issue during this entire middle stage of therapy is dependency, and the woman's struggle with her dependency needs in all relationships, including the therapy relationship. Women are thought of as dependent people. Dependency is associated with qualities such as clinging, helplessness and weakness. Women have been put into a position of being economically dependent within patriarchy, but the relationship between economic dependency and emotional dependency is not straightforward. Women are the emotional caretakers and nurturers. Men bring their emotional life to their wives. Although this is not made explicit within the relationship, men's dependency needs are more often met within marriage and their emotional worries are processed by their wives. No such equivalent place exists for women. As we have seen, women learn early on not to expect this kind of nurturance from a woman or a man, and so they come to protect themselves from their dependency needs.

Dependency needs remind a woman of her feelings of inadequacy and emptiness. The picture she must present to the world is of an adult woman, but inside she feels she is a child and her feelings of dependency painfully remind her of and confirm her smallness. The tension between women and men in heterosexual relationships often centres around this dynamic, with women alternately curbing and exposing their dependency needs and men being perplexed, angered, or intimidated by them [4]. As we look into this dynamic, a picture unfolds of both women and men being wary of women's dependency needs and of working together to suppress them.

In the clinical situation women reveal how they defend against these needs. They create a protective boundary between themselves and those to whom they wish to relate closely. They express the fear that if the little-girl emerges within intimate relationships then they will be only the little girl. The woman's shaky boundaries lead her to feel that somehow she will lose herself. That she will be taken over, that she will be subsumed in the other; or that the little girl inside will take over the other person – that they are too close. Women carry with them the feeling that their needs are completely overwhelming, unending, insatiable, bad, shameful. They feel their needs will drive other people away; many women say with distressing confidence that they will be rejected because of this needy part of themselves.

This happens in the therapy relationship as well. At one level we see an adult woman: but our therapy alerts us to the little-girl inside the woman, together with all the defences which hide her. It is this little girl inside who emerges time and time again, with woman after woman, in every therapy relationship that we have experienced so far. Now, as we know, women do not feel good about this little girl inside. Their critical view of her will be reflected in the judgemental way women describe their feelings. The woman feels that the therapist will reject the little girl inside, so she cannot expose her. There is a whole process that goes on step by step whereby the therapist responds to this little girl behind the defences, encourages her to come out into the relationship, reassures the client that she, the therapist, will not be overwhelmed by this little girl, is not afraid of her and does not feel that this part of the woman is bad, greedy and ugly (which is often what the woman fears). The client reacts in two ways during this process. On the one hand she feels tremendous potential: here at last is someone who may not reject her, who may really accept her, someone who may be able to respond to all these feelings that she has had so much difficulty with herself. On the other hand she is still cautious, because to let this little girl out openly within the therapy relationship and to admit to being close to and needing the therapist is an acknowledgement of dependency on another person.

Why are these feelings of dependency so terrifying? Why do they make the client so vulnerable and insecure? We need to look at the context in which women's egos develop, to find the answer. The very first relationship, that we all had, was one in which we were totally and utterly dependent for physical and emotional growth. In the first months of life as the ego is in the process of forming, there is not yet a sense of self. This state of helplessness and utter dependency, together with the original infantile state of early ego formation, is carried deep within our memory. This was a time when we were merged psychologically with mother. We did not have a sense of our own boundaries. In the process of ego development this sense of self develops and emerges through and because of the relationships the baby has with those around it. As the ego develops, so too does the sense of one's own and other people's boundaries. As we have seen, the mother identifies with her infant daughter and, because of her feelings about herself and her little-girl inside, transmits both a positive and a negative sense of self to her infant daughter. Mother has complex feelings about her own, and in turn her daughter's, emotional dependency needs. As a result there is that 'push and pull' between mother and daughter in their relationship. The little daughter comes to feel that somehow her emotional dependency needs are not acceptable. Because she feels this needy part of herself is not acceptable a split occurs in her ego whereby this dependent little-girl inside is hidden from the world. This split results in further deprivation for that little-girl inside. Because she is not in contact with others, she is not receiving the nourishment, the nurture, the contact, the love that is necessary for continued maturity and growth. There is, as we have seen, a second 'push' for the little girl when she has to try to give up her mother as her primary love object and attempt to turn this interest and expectation towards her father, who is the embodiment of all males, in order to achieve successful heterosexual socialization and sexual orientation. Both of these 'pushes' are experienced as rejection by mother and are central to this issue of women's dependency. Deeply buried inside a woman's psychology is the feeling that her dependency needs and therefore herself are not acceptable, that they will be met with rejection and pushed away yet again.

The woman brings all these feelings about the little-girl inside into the relationship with her therapist. In the therapy the client often fights to hide her fear that the therapist will not be able to accept and meet her needs. Women clients find it extremely painful to acknowledge their feelings of deprivation and consequent neediness. But the cornerstone of feminist therapy is to bring this conflict into the open, for as it is gradually exposed, the woman will come to understand more about what it is she searches for in her relationships. These dependency needs are central to the therapy relationship. The woman may feel tremendous guilt and shame about her dependency desires and try to push them away. She inevitably feels that it is inappropriate to have these needs and to want them to be understood and satisfied by the therapist. The therapist's job is to encourage the client to express the dependency desires in the therapy relationship. Frequently, a woman will say that in intimate relationships she is yearning for someone she can depend on, who can provide an emotional climate of security, yet at the same time allow her to remain an individual, her own person. Because one of her unconscious fears in an intimate relationship is that she will lose herself and become merged with her partner, and because she does not believe that anyone could allow her to be close *and separate* (including herself), the issue of dependency is conflictual.

As the neediness is allowed to emerge in the therapy relationship we discover that many women then feel the urge to take care of the therapist. At the point of being able to take in the therapist's caring, the woman may become caught up in worrying and fantasizing about the needs of the therapist. By exploring this dynamic in the transference relationship, a critical component of the mother–daughter relationship emerges. When the client takes in good feelings from another woman, she is experiencing an unusual emotional state of affairs. This may both please her and make her anxious. She may feel frightened that she will lose this new kind of caring. She may attempt to mobilize against this anxiety that the nurture produces by taking care of the therapist. She may feel she needs to take care of the therapist in order to keep her there. We feel that this is something that girls did with their mothers, and women continue to do with their mothers; in order to keep mother close to her in some way, a woman will become her mother's mother. Mother may have encouraged this out of her own need to be looked after.

Precisely because the client's life history has not prepared her to take in caring from another woman on a consistent basis she may find this situation hard to negotiate psychically. She may find herself involved in a series of what might be called tests, tests that are about coping with the contact in this relationship. She may express her fears by worrying that the therapist will not understand her, will disappoint her. Where real cases of disappointment arise in the therapy relationship as they are bound to, they have to be examined in their reality. The therapist must be able to explore with the client what this disappointment means: can the client accept that somebody with whom she has a relationship, who is giving to her, may disappoint, may make mistakes? The therapist must unravel the real issue: she must establish whether or not this disappointment is a defence against the belief that the therapist is there with her.

As women therapists the issue of disappointment in the therapy relationship brings us and our clients up against the image deep inside of all women, and men too, of women as either all-good, all-providing or all withholding and disappointing. When a client feels disappointed with the therapist, both she and the therapist may slot into this image of woman as inadequate. We have discussed earlier the time in a girl's life when she builds a world of internal relationships which are more manageable than the exterior world. She takes into herself two pictures of how mother could be: the all-good provider or the all-powerful withholder. These two images are not just pictures of mother; more significantly they are pictures of all women, of who the little girl can be. This internal split is also projected on to a female therapist, whom the client may experience as all-providing or all-withholding. It is most important within the context of this real relationship between the two women for them to reject the image of the therapist as either all-powerful or all-terrible and acknowledge instead that the therapist may sometimes disappoint.

Alongside the process of the woman client bringing her little-girl to therapy, unravelling her defences, runs another equally important process, what we might call the repair work. When we described the early development of the infant girl's ego, we discussed how she takes in the person of the mother, embodies it, and this in turn creates the self. In the therapy relationship a part of the client regresses, if you like, to this very early stage; the needy little-girl inside is now fed in the relating and the emotional contact with the therapist. This taking-in of caring from the therapist both heals the hurt of the little-girl and also provides the woman with a chance to embody the goodness of the therapist, to feel that goodness inside herself. When we say 'heal', in this instance we mean that the therapist allows the woman's pain and her previous loss to be acknowledged and validated. In allowing the pain, anger, loss, regret, despair etc, to emerge, the therapist and the client are transforming a deeply rooted internal experience. The therapist acknowledges the painful feeling as legitimate: the girl wanted to be loved and accepted; this wanting, not met, turned against the girl herself in her psyche, so she felt there to be something wrong with her, that she was to blame for not getting what she wanted. As the pain is exposed and tolerated this formulation dissolves. The woman puts her anger, her defences, her despair more outside. As she puts it outside herself, so she is allowing the therapist to come in with the goodness, love, nurturance, attention and care that she so badly wants. She is beginning to have a new experience of relating.

This process of the client embodying the nurture from the therapist is not without its problems and will be met with by the same kind of defences that we have seen before. The client may for example propose a false ending of therapy by claiming to be 'cured' when we know she is only just beginning to turn the corner. At a certain point when her internal object relations have begun to shift and she is embodying the love and caring of the therapist, she may become frightened. She is fearful that if she can really cope then she will not be entitled to continue to need and to be cared for by the therapist. What she is feeling is that she does not need the therapist in quite the same way as she did before. Some women feel they have to be absolutely desperate before they can ask for help, and be helped. So if a woman feels she is now coping, she fears she will lose her therapist and all that the therapist is giving her. Because the woman has within her memory and within her psychology the sense of having been pushed away in her relationship with mother, she fears that if she acknowledges that she has taken in something from the therapist, that she is a person in her own right, she will be pushed away yet again.

So at this point in the therapy we may see one of two things. First, the woman may suggest prematurely that she is ready to end therapy. This suggestion needs to be explored in detail and at length, because it could be easy at that point, especially if the therapist is feeling that the client is in fact much 'healthier', to accept at face value her proposal to end therapy. Yet it is just at this point that what must be explored is *why* the client is feeling that she is ready to leave. Is it because she fears she will be pushed away by the therapist? Is it because the relationship with the therapist is so precious to her that she feels very vulnerable? Perhaps she wants to cut herself off from it in order to have control over the anticipated loss.

The second thing we may see at this stage in therapy is that at a point where the therapist feels the client is much better, and the woman herself has acknowledged for some time that she is feeling better, in herself, suddenly it is as if the woman takes ten steps back. She presents herself as having lost the ability to cope once again; she does not understand why this has happened, but it has happened. At this point we would explore with the woman why feeling good within herself was so frightening. We would ask her to go back a couple of weeks and try to remember what it was like to feel that she was coping. We would ask her if there was anything frightening about those feelings. It is highly probable that the woman felt very frightened or nervous since, if she felt better within herself, she imagined she would have to leave the therapy. And so her unconscious reaction is, 'I can't cope,' which is a way of saying, 'I still need you. And I'm afraid that if I need you less and if I can cope then you won't let me be here with you.'

Another defence at this stage of the therapy may be the client saying that she does not like the therapist, or finds her difficult or unperceptive; or she may feel that the therapist does not really want to give to her at all. She may be a very 'difficult' client at this point; she may be protecting so hard that every move the therapist makes towards her is met with, 'You're not doing enough,' 'You're not doing it right,' 'You don't really like me,'

'I'm sure you don't really want to see me at five o'clock,' 'I'm sure you're only forcing that smile when you see me!' 'I'm sure you can't wait till the end of the session,' or alternatively, 'I can't make today's appointment, my car just broke down.' The therapist may find that she actually has to 'chase' the client within the therapy session. It is very important for the therapist to monitor what happens during this very difficult period for both women, because if she is working with a woman who is particularly deprived, she may too be tempted to pull out of the relationship because of the strains on her as a therapist, and that is precisely what must not be communicated to the client.

These reactions may all seem paradoxical. The client wanted to feel good within herself, so why do these changes bring up confusing and frightening feelings? She feels sure she may lose more than she will gain. The new changes within herself are unfamiliar and she cannot rely on them yet. As a result of her changing, many facets of her relationships will also have to change and this can produce tension. The client will feel a tremendous relief that all these issues can be discussed and worked through in the therapy.

The issues that a woman brings to therapy, her dependency needs, her defences and the therapist's response to them are part and parcel of the middle phase of the therapy relationship.

IV The Feminist Psychotherapy Relationship: Ending and Separating; Issues for the Psychotherapist

Ending and Separating

In the course of therapy, then, the woman has had a chance to explore the themes of her inner life in a new way. She has encountered a particular kind of support for exploring personal issues, an encouragement to clarify what is important, conflictual, painful and so on for her. Real-life events may have changed and certainly the woman's perception of herself will have altered. At the same time another process is going on which is that the client comes to experience the nurturing of the therapist. The two women have real contact and a real relationship, which allows the client to take in and embody the nurturing aspects of the therapist. Both these simultaneous experiences promote a feeling of well-being and provide for more integration of the ego. Precisely because the woman's internal world is changing, she comes to be more self-accepting, and less of her is hidden away.

She is in turn able to experience feeling loved, and experience herself as being lovable, as being entitled to nurturance, as entitled to contact, as worthy of good things, as worthy of living her own life. This process of feeling that the little girl inside is accepted, understood and loved by the therapist is an extremely important part of the healing process.

Throughout the process of therapy the woman is experimenting with ways of showing who she is, of bringing her little girl, her needs and her vulnerabilities into safe relationships in the world outside therapy. What the therapist sees, and what the client is experiencing for herself, is a reduction in the discrepancy between the woman, or the part of the woman who comes into therapy, and the part of the woman who is out in the world. The therapist has encouraged the woman to bring her little girl into the therapy relationship and also into other relationships with friends, with lovers and so on. This interaction in other social relationships helps to integrate the little-girl part into the whole ego of the woman. The woman brings back her experiences outside therapy for discussion with the therapist, and together they explore what it feels like for the woman to feel more whole and complete in the outside world.

As the little-girl part is accepted and integrated by the woman, by her therapist, friends and lover(s), she then experiences herself being listened to, fed and nurtured. She no longer feels herself to be a screaming mass of unending needs. She feels less insatiable, less needy and less ravenous. She feels less judgemental of herself, less anxious and less critical. She trusts that she knows herself more and therefore can relate more directly. She has a reasonable expectation that her needs and who she is will be taken into account by others: the therapist and client have, together, been building the woman's sense of self. Now the woman can be herself, all of herself, wherever she is. At an internal level she has a continuity of experience. She no longer becomes the person she feels others want her to be. She no longer compulsively adapts her personality to fit the needs of others in order to feel accepted. She reflects instead her own sense of being all right and secure within herself and meets situations and relationships with this new substantive feeling.

The feeding, acceptance and transformation of the little girl makes for a change in her internal object relations. This change at the psychic structural level means that the woman's dependency needs change. She does not need the therapist, she does not need her lover, she does not need her children, she does not need her friends in precisely the same way. She does not need to be connected to them in order to have a self. She does not acquire her sense of self through them. She has a self. Her little girl has had a chance to be engaged with and integrated, and she can now relate as a whole person, who like all human beings is dependent and interdependent on others. This is very important because the end of therapy or successful therapy does not in any sense preclude being dependent on people. To be autonomous, to have a sense of self, to feel nurtured, to feel less insatiable, does not mean that one does not have needs; what it does mean is that the basis of the needs has shifted, and that opens up the possibility that they can actually be met.

At the point in therapy when the woman begins to feel that she is no longer needing her therapist in the same way and begins to experience a change in herself in relation to her therapy, it may no longer seem to make sense in the same way as it did before. She is experiencing herself in other relationships outside therapy and she is enjoying what she experiences. She feels her autonomy. So she may begin to suggest to the therapist, in all sorts of different ways, the idea of separating from her and ending the therapy.

When the woman does bring up the possibility of separating from the therapist and ending the therapy, she may fear two things. First, she may fear the therapist will not support her autonomy and her strength. She fears her disapproval. Second, she may imagine that she is stirring up feelings of competition and envy on the part of the therapist who will in some way want to hold her back. She may anticipate that somehow her good feelings about herself will threaten the therapist. This is in itself an issue to work on in the therapy relationship. For women, because of the ambivalences of the mother–daughter relationship, have not had the experience of feeling their strength and separateness supported. Women have often shared and felt equal and close in their distress, lack of confidence, insecurities and so on. But it is very difficult and unusual for women to feel equal with each other in their strengths without allied feelings of competition and envy. It is extremely important to talk about these fears of competition or envy, of the anticipated disapproval of the therapist, and to go through the woman's wishes for separation in great detail during the course of separation.

At the beginning of the therapy relationship there was an inequality, in terms of vulnerability and neediness in the therapy situation. In the course of the therapy this power relation has shifted and the woman, through her own integration of her little girl, now feels an adult and more equal with her therapist. Now the woman is exploring yet another level of acceptance. She struggles to feel this new kind of support. She takes in her therapist's acceptance of this new way of her being.

The second thing that the woman may be fearing as she brings up the idea of separation and ending the therapy is that somehow she will be rejecting the therapist, and making her feel inadequate. She feels as if she is saying 'I'm rejecting what it is that you still have to give to me, I don't need that any more,' and that this belittles or diminishes what the therapist has to give. In her anxiety about upsetting the therapist she may want to reassure her that she does still need her. We have discussed this dynamic within the mother–daughter relationship, where separation on the part of the daughter both makes the daughter anxious and is difficult for the mother as well, because as the daughter tries to separate from mother, mother fears the loss of her sense of self. In the therapy relationship we find the client caught up in reassuring the therapist that she still needs her. As the client feels more able to cope and as she tries to separate from her therapist, the woman simultaneously seeks to reassure the therapist that she is still needed, that she is not going to be abandoned. She does this by presenting her with new problems to be worked on in the therapy. But this is in itself the very problem. In our experience it is often very difficult for a woman to accept that the therapist does support and approve of her wish for separation.

Another issue which frequently emerges during this separation process centres on the woman's gradual awareness of the differences between herself and her therapist. As the woman increasingly experiences her therapist as a separate person, not someone whose primary function is as provider to the client, so she gradually begins to experience more of the therapist's personality and opinions. Her internal object relations have changed and she now has true boundaries and the confidence which enables her to feel that she and her therapist can work together towards an understanding without that understanding requiring that they be in unison. Different views her therapist may express which at an earlier time in the therapy may have been deeply distressing and threatening for the woman take on a different meaning. Now the separateness which these differing views symbolize can be tolerated as the woman can be both in relationship with and separate from her therapist.

An important part of the separation process in feminist therapy is to ensure that the client does not feel that separation from the therapist will mean that she must contain and cope with all of her needs on her own, that she cannot bring her needs to others. It is for this reason that we have come to believe that it is important for the therapist to remain available as a therapist to the client after the therapy has ended. Even though the woman has embodied the therapist and the experiences of their relationship will thus live on inside her, nevertheless it is vital for the woman to feel that the therapist continues to be someone she can reach out to if and when the need arises. A woman leaving therapy must not experience a repetition of her earlier 'push away' from and loss of mother; separating from a feminist therapist must not mean that when she loses her therapist she loses her for life. The ability to be autonomous does not mean she will no longer have a woman who will love and support her. One of our clients when ending her therapy said, 'Somehow it feels like a love affair, a good love affair that's ending, and that doesn't make sense because you don't leave a love affair that's working very well.' Feminist therapy is about learning to love the little girl inside that patriarchy has taught us to despise; it is about allowing her to grow up and become autonomous; above all it is about being loved by another woman and helped by her to grow and become separate.

This process of therapy and the model we have been describing, then, are informed by the theoretical understanding of women's psychological development as outlined in Chapter 2. This theory suggests new ways of understanding the content, the transference and the real relationship between the two people engaged in therapy together. This new understanding provides the beginnings to a theory about the practice of a feminist psychoanalysis.

Issues for the Psychotherapist

The analysis we employ to understand the lives and psychic conflicts of our clients applies equally to ourselves as therapists. As women working with women we may hear what the client says and what we judge to be in the transference almost as replays of our own daughter–mother, mother–daughter relationship. This is not necessarily countertransference, for it is the attitude and stance we adopt towards hearing our own lives spread out before us by our clients that makes for helpful therapy. It is inevitable that as women who have shared the same socialization process, we will find many points of identification with our women clients. We were all little girls who were taught to be women; we all have little girls inside us; we all share on some level the same struggle for self-actualization; we all feel anger at the individual and social position of women. Therefore, frequently we will identify strongly with the women with whom we work. To scrutinize our emotional responses to our clients requires a particular sensitivity on the part of feminist psychotherapists who must distinguish between countertransference issues, identification and empathy.

The client will inevitably trigger in the therapist conflicts in her own life. Unless the therapist is sufficiently aware of these conflicts, and her attitudes, prejudices and blind spots, she may attempt to use the therapy to satisfy her own needs. To minimize the therapist acting on her unconscious processes (countertransference) all therapists go through intensive psychotherapy themselves. This should ensure that the psychotherapist can distinguish between her needs and the client's needs in the therapy and be unambiguously available to the client within the therapy setting. Since no training analysis can claim to have exposed every nook and cranny of the psyche, or to have worked through every troublesome issue in the therapist's life, it is important that the therapist be alert to the feelings that the client sparks off in her. Without constant monitoring of her own feelings and being aware of countertransference issues the therapist may offer interpretations or direct the client's interest in areas that have more meaning for her than for the client. The therapist's own analysis is then the first protection against abuse. Feminist therapy acknowledges the material and structural basis of the distress of individual women and recognizes that the psychological development of female therapists will in no measure be substantially different from that of their women clients. Clinical meetings and supervision [1] groups in which therapists can think through their reactions to people with whom they are working also provide support for the therapist and are as important a part of training as the therapist's own therapy. We prescribe for ourselves as therapists the very same contexts we sought as women trying to break our isolation, i.e. consciousness-raising groups for practising therapists. These groups encourage therapists to discuss issues while *identifying* with their women clients.

Our identification is one of the burdens of being a therapist. We hear the stories of all our lives – lives of oppression, pain, compromise, disappointment, frustration, unexpressed rage and staggering bravery – much of which stems from the sexual arrangements within patriarchy, distilled through the individual nuclear family. As therapists we need a place to let off steam, so to speak, to clarify our emotional reactions and work out the connections between the emotional issues which confront us daily in our work and the underlying social issues, and to see how these relate to psychological phenomena and the work of therapy. Ideally, the supervision setting could integrate this dimension.

However, we do not necessarily find it of therapeutic value to share these identifications with clients, except perhaps in the most general way in the initial stages of deciding to do therapy together. We do not think that it serves a positive function to disclose our own experiences to our clients, for several reasons. First, it becomes a burden to the client, who now has actual information that she may use in an attempt to care *for* the therapist, be concerned *for* the therapist, rather than examining the difficulties of her being in therapy for herself. Second, revelations of the therapist's personal experience may serve to cut short what is in the client's mind, again distracting her from her own experiences. Therapy should provide a place for a woman to explore her own experiences away from the need to respond to others. Third, while as therapists we provide a model for autonomy, we do not wish to encourage our clients to over-identify with us so that they then have yet another struggle to free themselves from the imitation of a new authority figure. Lastly, self-disclosure by the therapist would serve to cut off and interrupt the transference projections of the client that are an essential aspect of the therapy relationship and process. However, since women's experience is structurally isolated and many women will feel a great deal of support by hearing that other women's lives are similar, we encourage and create therapy situations in which experiences can be shared, such as group-therapy settings, topics workshops (see Chapter 5) and, of course, consciousness-raising groups.

The therapist must be able to empathize with the initial concerns of the client and would do well to remind herself of her own first therapy appointment and the range of feelings that accompanied it – vulnerability, hope, fear. If the therapist agrees to do therapy with a woman, she is opening herself up to a serious new relationship which will encompass intimacy and tenderness on both sides as the therapy proceeds.

The therapist and the client are working together to try to understand the client's emotional distress. The therapist, outside the client's actual confusing or tortured experience, is like an emotional buoy, supporting the client in her struggle to come through the repeating patterns of stress. The therapist must be able to view what the client is sharing with her from a non-judgemental position, because a significant part of the curative process is to help clients break through the shame that accompanies their thoughts, feelings, fantasies and desires, as a prelude to working through the difficult themes. However, the ability of the therapist to provide the appropriate environment for the client inevitably raises the issue of the power relationship in the therapy.

To begin with the therapist is seen as powerful because she aids the client: this dependency has its allied feelings of powerlessness and helplessness. We have seen how in the transference relationship the feelings and attitudes the client learned in infancy from her caretaker come up for examination. But these are not only of concern within the scope of the transference, because it is not the client's psychic imaginings which suggest that she is more vulnerable and less powerful than the therapist; there is a real power differential in the therapy relationship. The contract in therapy is that, first, both client and therapist are committed to using the energy and skills at hand to understand and work through the psychic distress of the client. Second, the client at various stages of the therapy will feel more or less acutely her need for the therapist. The therapist does not have a parallel need for the client, however much she may enjoy working with a particular woman. Third, the therapist's confidence about the task that confronts her means that she is bringing a different part of herself to the therapy situation from the client – she does not show her vulnerability. Lastly, although there are many additional ways in which this power differential is manifested, it is the therapist who makes the interpretations and seems to have an overview of the client's psyche. This is indeed a powerful position to be in in relation to another.

The client will have a range of feelings about this power differential and it is important for the therapist to be clean about this dynamic so that she can help the client to explore the quite understandable fears and anxieties she may have about potential abuse within this setting. The therapist should not deny the power she has. Women have been consistently tampered with by authority figures and their caution and concern about what may be done to them as clients is legitimate and based on social reality. Worries about the power differential may find their place for discussion at various stages within the therapy and it will be important to sort through with the client the various levels and meanings of her feelings of vulnerability. At times it may be important to validate that her vulnerability is real and that the therapist and client are in different positions within their relationship.

One way of minimizing the power differential is to demystify aspects of the therapy relationship. As the client is able to understand the background to the confusing emotional states she is in, so she will be alerted to her own voice and strength; a shared language and understanding of psychological affairs. There is no need for a therapist to withhold information about what she understands of the client's psychic processes if it would give the woman more sense of perspective and understanding of herself and the therapy process.

The therapist should be open to talking about her theoretical biases, her prejudices and how her theory and practice view the psychology of women so that the client is aware of what sort of therapy she is committing herself to. *All therapies are informed by a political perspective.* Ideas about the psyche are thought about in particular ways. Many psychotherapists often make the mistake of offering up their clinical work as though it were value-free. In this sense they are unconscious of how a political view of the world shapes a psychological view of women and how this in turn will provide a particular viewpoint. As feminist psychotherapists we bring in our political and personal attitudes, biases and values to the work we do. We hear what our clients say with a particular ear, no more special in its particularity than other therapists, but with a stated bias that sees women as the oppressed sex within patriarchy.

From our point of view feminist therapists must believe in a person's open choice of sexual partner. Because of the history and the continuing discrimination against homosexuality in the psychiatric professions it has often been impossible for lesbians to seek psychotherapy. This has been the case both for the lesbian in search of individual psychotherapy as well as for lesbian couples seeking counselling. Feminist therapists need to examine their own deeply held views and possible fears about lesbianism (even if one is a lesbian and a therapist) in order to work in a clear and unprejudiced way with lesbian clients. Feminist therapists must examine and discuss issues of sexuality within the therapy relationship with both heterosexual and lesbian clients.

Attitudes about class, both conscious and unconscious, are inevitably felt in the therapy relationship (even where the class background of therapist and client are similar) [2]. There may be tension on either side about this, and a tendency on the part of the therapist to see issues which may well have to do with class only in terms of intra-psychic conflict (this may derive from the failure by the training institutions to give adequate consideration to class). Class is important to who we are, as, of course, is cultural and ethnic background, and often serves to prohibit certain activities unless one is from the appropriate background (this is much more obviously so in the United Kingdom than the United States) and a therapist must maintain an awareness of how class affects her and her view of her clients and be ready to explore with the client how and what class means in her life at both a material and a psychological level.

It is vital for the therapist to care for and respect the women she works with. We sense that much training instils in the therapist a sense of superiority over the client, which is revealed in the way many cases are discussed in clinical seminars and papers. We feel this arises for the following reason. The therapist undoubtedly feels quite genuine concern and sometimes distress at the plight of her client, even when she feels she can be an effective progressive force in her life. The taking in of others' painful experiences puts enormous emotional pressure on the therapist and this is compounded by the therapeutic situation as it does not allow the therapist to share and thus discharge some of her reactions. Instead, she is offered two options: she is encouraged to analyse her emotional reactions to her clients within the context of countertransference or offered a highly evolved diagnostic scheme with a specialist vocabulary into which to fit her clients. These two options are valuable and should not necessarily be jettisoned by progressive therapists. What we are concerned with is that these two mechanisms become the conveyor belt for a change in attitude on the part of the therapist from wholesome compassion to faint contempt and alienation for people she sees in therapy. There have been several interesting attempts by feminist therapists to form groups to discuss many of these issues [3].

In addition to a supervisory or consciousness-raising group, we have found it useful to discuss topics of concern to feminist therapists. For example, a dilemma that confronts us in a particularly stark way is that of how to avoid reproducing the ideological stick of 'good mother' in our role as the professional 'good mother'. Does not the professionalization of women's 'giving' skills reach its apex in being a good therapist? Is there not a striking parallel between female socialization and a job in the 'helping profession' as a therapist? Both roles require women to help relieve the distress of others, albeit by very different methods.

A way to work on such dilemmas is to discuss them with others who experience them. In turn, this provides for a kind of nurturance which goes against the classic feminine role of giving to the world. For it is essential that as feminist therapists we can find our own sources of support and nurturance.

Women's Theme-Centred Workshops
and Psychodynamic Therapy Groups

Theme-Centred Workshops

At the Women's Therapy Centre we have led a variety of theme-centred groups for women on topics that emerged in individual therapy sessions, in our staff supervision and study groups, which struck us as useful for women to work on in a group situation. These topic workshops are of short duration, lasting for two to eight sessions. The women who enrol are not pre-selected and vary enormously in terms of their experience in therapy groups. Some have never participated in a group or workshop before, some turn up regularly in the Women's Therapy Centre workshops and others have been regular members of ongoing psychotherapy groups. The majority are between twenty-five and forty-five years old, but there are many older and some younger women who come along. Class background includes women from working-class backgrounds, first-generation 'educated' women and middle-class women, with a wide distribution in income [1]. The ethnic and national backgrounds are mixed but with a striking absence of Asian, Black and Greek women (this we think is because there is no Third World woman or first-generation Greek woman offering such a group as the Women's Therapy Centre). Some of the women who participated in these groups are themselves self-consciously feminists, while at least half of the women do not see themselves in that way. An exciting observation is that, not withstanding the heterogeneous nature of the women involved, the issues that come up for all of them, young or old, married, single, working outside the home or not etc. resonate at a psychological level. Women's experience, as we have discussed before, is both individually experienced and structurally isolated.

The topics themselves range from dependency, competition, sexuality, mothers and daughters, anger, and jealousy, to issues around power, difficulties in intimate relationships, giving and receiving, compulsive eating, and anorexia [2]. In all these workshops the emphasis has been on exploring painful and complicated themes with a view to enriching one's understanding of the underlying dynamics in each woman's individual psychology as well as opening up space for a new relationship to the issue to emerge.

71

The group workshops are structured differently from the individual therapy sessions, with perhaps an initial exposition by the workshop leader on why this particular topic is a problem area for women, a tour of the room so that participants can share their reasons for coming, followed by an exercise – often a guided fantasy – designed to uncover the issues for each woman involved [3]. The group would continue by both individual work with the participants, general discussion, role play, and homework designed to help the individual women think through a new position to the problem theme when encountering it. The workshops, then, are designed not simply to open up issues but to provide new solutions.

Much of what we have learnt about women's psychology in the workshop setting has confirmed what we were seeing in our individual sessions. Neither experience substitutes for the other: workshop groups and individual sessions all serve different purposes. Because in a theoretical sense the work dovetails, here we will just point to the value of these workshops, why we see them as useful and discuss in some detail themes from several of them – competition, anger, giving and receiving – as these are important issues in the lives of women.

Being in a group with other women itself may be a novel experience. Many women have never spent intentional time together, time in which they can both reflect and be active in relation to their experience. Much of women's time is, of course, spent with other women, but in contexts that women may not have chosen themselves, and that therefore do not have the same meaning [4]. Because of this self-determined way of coming together the women in the group have a new experience of being with other women. In making contact with each other and working together at a psychological level, the process of valuing each other and themselves starts. Women are, in a myriad of overt and subtle ways, discouraged from taking themselves or their experience seriously. In sharing together in the workshop women are in fact taking each other's experiences seriously. In turn this reflects back on each individual woman in the room, for as she notices the contribution others make, so she can begin to conceive that her presence, her opening up aspects of herself, her interventions and so on are of value. The insights that come out of such workshops are of special significance, because they are born out of women sharing and exploring together, revealing intimate aspects of their internal experiences and discovering how much they have in common beneath the surface. This coming together is an important step in breaking one's isolation. Through sharing in a safe environment aspects of one's experience, one discovers that other women feel similarly and can identify with aspects of one's life. It is often the feeling of isolation that women experience added to their actual isolation in the home and in individual relationships that creates a tremendous amount of psychic distress. This new way of coming together [5] transforms a repeated pattern in women's lives. It is a challenge and opens up the door to further exploration and possibilities. Twelve women sitting together focusing on a theme in their lives is a dramatic, tender, upsetting and inspiring experience. Many workshops have a certain electricity as the women painfully build together a picture of their lives at a psychological level.

As we have discussed earlier, because of their psychosocial development, women have come to be attentive, supportive and often 'appropriate good givers'. The positive aspects of this giving can make for a very nurturing group in which women take in the caring from other women. Coming to a group is in itself an exposure and can be somewhat nerve-racking at first, for one may have feelings of trepidation as to what will be uncovered and revealed and other participants' issues may spark one off in unanticipated directions. Within these workshops, precisely because of women's capacity to give [6], there is often an atmosphere of tremendous tenderness, caring and concern which forms an important security blanket for all the members, in turn creating a safe climate so that issues in each individual woman's psychology can be explored.

Related to this psychological skill of giving is women's ability to 'tune in' to others, to be able to pick up the nuances and significance of others' experience. Her emotional antennae help her imagine what another woman in telling her story is feeling. For a woman to be so immediately understood by all the women in the group, or even a large proportion of them, is tremendously helpful and very reassuring. Not that such understanding should in any way curtail her from exploring, articulating and expressing the parts that people do not understand, but when she says, 'My husband was talking to a woman at a party for a long time and I felt I shouldn't feel jealous, there was nothing really to be jealous of, but I did feel jealous,' she gets an immediate and empathetic understanding which then allows the other women to explore with her (and of course for themselves) why that should be such an uncomfortable and upsetting situation. She does not have to explain first to the group that it is upsetting – they all understand and know from their own identification and shared feelings.

Two other factors make a workshop an extremely productive setting. The very fact that there is a topic workshop on a theme that a woman relates to as something she experiences in her own life (and something which she would like some help with), reduces the shame and embarrassment that attaches to feelings such as competition, jealousy, envy and anger. It opens up the possibility that one can look at such feelings, that perhaps they need not be so threatening in the first place. Women thus come to a workshop with a certain eagerness to engage with the topic. In addition, because the workshop participants are not entwined with each other and because the limited time for the group to meet reduces the transference manifestations which are so much a part of the working-through process of the psychodynamic therapy group, there is a sensitivity and a support for each woman's struggle.

Now that we have described the background to the workshops we turn to discuss the content of particular topic groups.

Women come to a workshop on competition with many different kinds of feelings which they call competitive. In consciousness-raising groups women discussed openly for the first time the destructive nature of competition between women and how women are frequently caught in the cycle of competing with each other for men. In the consciousness-raising group women came to be critical and angry at the society and of course at individual men who promote the competition. Important breakthroughs about the need to support other women reduced the threatened feelings, thus producing important changes in women's consciousness. However, so deep, so dangerous and now so shameful were competitive feelings that issues of competition among women within consciousness-raising groups stayed hidden beneath the surface. Many of these uncomfortable feelings were kept outside the group and subsequently led to the dissolution of many groups. We have noticed in our clinical work how difficult it is, particularly for a self-conscious feminist, to admit to having competitive feelings towards other women. She will often respond to these feelings with self-punishment and shame. These feelings confirm for her that she is not as strong, self-confident and independent as she 'should' be. In the workshop it is very reassuring for women to have a place to discuss these feelings, to experience them, while the therapist provides the safety net so that the feelings can come out rather than stay hidden under the surface and remain threatening as they do so often in women's relationships with each other.

One of the important and most obvious ways in which competition between women is expressed is, of course, in the sexual arena. As we saw earlier, one of the social requirements for a woman is that she must be allied with a man, from whom she will derive her social and personal value (and hence her self-esteem); furthermore, she has come to see herself as others see her. This critical view she has of herself she extends to other women both as a comparison and as a threat. We know that when a woman walks into a room full of people she automatically evaluates the other women, and unwittingly ranks herself against them. After the initial physical impression she will take in other attributes of the women she is evaluating – their intellectual activity, their job, their sexual arrangements and so on. This may sound crude and unpleasant, as indeed the experience itself is. Women look at other women who seem suitably 'attractive' and imagine that they are comfortable and easy with themselves; each woman wonders how the other has achieved this self-assurance and envies and admires her. Each individual woman may feel depression or self-hate and hopelessness in relation to the others, while at the same time she may long to be in their shoes. Feelings of competition cover the deeper feelings of insecurity we have discussed earlier. The competitive feelings then add yet a new set of feelings of failure, lack of confidence and inadequacy. Perhaps the most painful aspect of this cycle of insecurity and competition is that women experience these feelings individually and yet they are common to millions of women.

In the exploration in the workshop the shame and isolation attached to such feelings begin to ease. Once accepted, the complexities around this psychological theme can be opened up.

We not only see competition among women in the pursuit of self-esteem, we also see competitive feelings which arise when a woman adopts and satisfies ambitions that lie outside those socially prescribed for women. When a woman is struggling to fulfil herself by living and working as fully as possible she may experience feelings of disloyalty, guilt and betrayal towards other women. She feels as though she is rejecting an image of femininity deep inside her – divorcing herself from other women. Other women in the group may admit to competitive feelings towards such a woman. An interesting example from a six-session workshop on competition illustrates these dynamics. One of the women, after enrolling for the group but before the first session, made a tape of a song she had written to sell. [7] In the first meeting she mentioned her hopes and fears about her desire to be a professional songwriter and everybody was very encouraging. She came to the second group meeting with news that it had been sold. She felt complicated about it, she said, because her flat mate was having a difficult time in her work as a dancer. She was not getting any parts. The songwriter did not know how to put together her good feelings about her success and her upset for her girl-friend's situation. In the group we discussed the unconscious psychological dilemma that ensues when one receives something one wants. Her difficulty with holding her success combined together with her friend's feelings of envy. The songwriter tried to push away her own conflicts about digesting her success by focusing on the envy of others. We explored the consequences of her sitting with her own success and how she and her friend could cope together with the difference in their experience without her having to deny or erase the good that was happening for her.

We frequently see how these competitive feelings serve to keep women in their place. Deeply instilled in each woman is the unconscious knowledge of the threshold that she may not cross in the attempt to fulfil herself. If she does she will have to contend with the anger and envy of other women. In this way women unconsciously collude to keep each other down. Patriarchy is distilled in each woman's psychology. Competitive and envious feelings keep women in line and prevent them from trying to get what they need in a society which has so many prohibitions. The woman herself keeps internal restraints which then serve to 'protect' her from her wants. Her guilt at the very desire keeps her unconsciously connected to the cultural image of femininity. She does not dare break ranks and be separate.

If we examine any form of oppression and deprivation, any situation in which there are those who have and those who have not, there are bound to be envious feelings. In our workshop on competition women discuss how the concomitant feelings of envy are ugly and uncomfortable. The woman who feels herself to be successful fears the envy of other women, because she herself is in touch with her envy of other women. In the workshop the cycle of desire changing to admiration, to envy and back to desire can be examined, because each woman will be at a different point in the cycle.

In our workshop we have discussed how feelings of guilt, envy and competition are closely linked. Women often feel guilty about feeling envious, and about wanting things for themselves. Guilt has a bad taste and feels disabling. It is a psychological mechanism in the service of the problem of connectedness and separateness for women. A woman who feels guilty about not wanting to visit her mother is expressing just this dilemma, as is the woman who feels the guilt when asserting her own needs and desires. In this sense guilt is a chain that binds one to another out of the impossibility of separateness. Women are attuned to other people's needs; they identify strongly with them; they feel they must respond to them. For them to assert their own needs, to say no, is a problem and makes them feel as though they are pushing another away. If a woman struggles for her autonomy to mark out her own boundaries, she may feel as though she is deserting, rejecting, or hurting others: she feels guilty. Because women's boundaries and separateness are unclear, women are particularly susceptible to these feelings of guilt. Guilt therefore, like feelings of competition and envy, blurs a central issue in women's psychology – that of psychological non-separateness and separateness.

Anger, of course, is another emotion which is a direct response to oppression; attempts are always made to diffuse the anger of oppressed people and substitute it with self-hatred and low self-esteem. Women are discouraged from expressing or having angry feelings. (See Chapters 1 and 2 for developmental descriptions of anger.) As a result women have much difficulty with this emotion. They find it ugly, they are scared that their anger will hurt others, they are ashamed of it, they find it hard to express, they fear it in others and so on. In our explorations we discover just how complex this emotion is. At one level it is empowering to be able to handle one's anger and express it appropriately. The workshop can provide a support for work on the acceptance of and expression of angry feelings. Women will all be inevitably at different stages in coping with anger and in expressing and understanding their angry feelings. This continuum can be very helpful to all the participants inasmuch as many women fear that if they let their anger out it would be very explosive. In the group they can watch other women express their anger and see that although it is frightening it can be managed.

Anger can be a straightforward and direct emotional communication between people. But like the other emotions we have discussed, of envy, guilt and competitiveness, so too can anger be understood in a more complex way as a defence. We have observed frequently how a denial of anger or a persistent holding on to angry feelings towards another is connected to the themes (in women's psychology) of deprivation and lack of separateness. Behind feelings of anger lie even more painful feelings of disappointment and despair. Not exposing the anger and disappointment stokes the fantasy that the other can make it all better. The anger keeps the connection. It fuels the hope that the person one is angry with will actually come through.

Another workshop addresses the theme of giving and receiving for women. All women know that in order to receive they must give. Giving is something a woman learns from early on; it is a survival tool; it is a deeply rooted part of her psychic structure and experience of self; it is the price she pays for economic security. But, as we have discussed already, a woman unconsciously feels that deep inside she has only a hungry part of herself which wants to take; she feels that she does not have anything to give. As we have said before, this wanting is so well defended against that one of the ways it plays out in life and, of course, in the group itself is through the feeling that the woman has that she is unjustified in receiving attention. In the group as in the outside world, only after a woman has given something to the other women does she feel justified in taking. If someone gives to her, is kind, concerned and receptive, for example, the woman feels the urge to repay: 'It's so lovely when the group listens to me, it helps me sort through my confusions. I feel perhaps you don't really all want to be so patient, and even while you're all paying attention to me I feel worried.' Being given to purely because she is deserving is often a confusing and moving moment for a woman because she does not conceive of herself in this way. She so anticipates annoyance and rejection by other group members that being given attention takes her by surprise.

A woman who experiences being given to when she feels she has not given first or will not have the opportunity to return the giving may react in another way. She may feel mistrustful of the other members of the group; the possibility that the group's attention is there simply because she is entitled never crosses her mind. In the group many women are feeling this at the same time. Because it is something that women share they have a chance to change this experience of giving and receiving.

One of the consequences of this painful and complicated dynamic of giving and receiving can be seen in women's experience of sex. Paradoxically, many women report a fear of being satisfied and given to. When there is a chance for their own needs to be met it is so unfamiliar that it may produce conflict (we can understand this if we refer back to the idea that women must defer to others' needs). Even when the opportunity presents itself, if there is a willing and giving lover, it may be terribly difficult for a woman to ask for or take sexual pleasure. Many women find it easier to give sexual pleasure to a partner. Receiving feels like too much is being given. A woman is often caught in a double bind; on the one hand she finds it difficult to assert her needs and yet deep down she may feel resentful that she is not being given to. She may feel anger at both herself and her lover for the situation in which she is preoccupied with satisfying his/her needs and not her own. The workshop helps the woman in her struggle to be able to experience receiving with pleasure instead of guilt.

It is precisely because of these points that we see the particular value of workshops and time-limited groups for women. Not only do the topics chosen relate directly to women's experience but also being in a single-sex group provides for the dynamics we have discussed [8]. These groups then reveal aspects of women's emotional lives which stand in direct contradiction to the stereotyped views of women and expose the hidden store of difficult and painful emotions – competitiveness, guilt, anger, envy, giving and receiving – that are the price of woman's outside face in the world.

Women's Psychodynamic Therapy Groups

The ongoing psychodynamic therapy groups which we now discuss involve six to ten women group members and one or two psychotherapists. Each of the women will have made a commitment to either a one-year group or an open-ended analytic group, and will have had an intake consultation with the therapist(s) in advance. Psychodynamic groups, unlike workshops, focus on interactions among participants and the dynamics of the group process. In individual open-ended therapy we saw that the relationship is a critical feature, and this is the case too in groups where the relationships between group members and members and the therapist are very important.

The therapist is made aware of the vast amount of need from the first meeting onwards. It is a critical dynamic in the group from which many other dynamics spring.

At the beginning of a group there is enormous anxiety by each woman about there 'not being enough' in the group. This may be expressed as there not being enough time, (one and a half or two hours), in silences and difficulties in being able to 'use' the time in the group, or in a series of references to other situations where the woman feels unsatisfied, frustrated, misunderstood, cut short etc. The therapist interprets her awareness of the underlying anxieties that group members have about whether the group can be a consistent and safe place for participants to be understood and to bring their needs.

Just as we have seen in both the workshops and individual therapy, there is an acute awareness on the part of each group member of the needs of the *other* women in the group. Each member is a woman with a woman's psychology and so her antennae enter the group with her. And so we encounter a second major dynamic which finds a group member trapped in conflict. That is, how can she take space and get help within the group when there is so much need around her? How can she take time in group without coming away feeling worried that she had taken 'too much'; guilty for receiving attention and nurturance and feeling that this 'getting' on her part 'took away' from the other women; frightened that her floodgates had started to open and her feelings would now overwhelm her (and perhaps the group); worried that the other group members feel angry with her for being so 'greedy'; worried that group members feel envy towards her for having the attention and care of the therapist.

As a result of these conflicts we see specific dynamics unfold in relation to the therapist. The very presence of the therapist in the group in some sense exposes the neediness that exists in the room at the same time as providing the safety for its exposure. As we have seen in other situations, women may try to hide their neediness, their little-girls inside. But being in a therapy group is in itself a step towards vulnerability, a statement that one does have needs. Women in the group may cope with the internal tensions produced by the presence of the therapist (a potential nurturer and satisfier) by trying to keep her out. The group may form a tentative alliance, putting the therapist just outside. Interventions, interpretations which the therapist offers may be met with caution and fear. Each woman and then the group as a whole tries to contain the need, and the group itself reproduces the false boundaries between the needs and the group. The therapist represents a breaker of these false boundaries as well as a potential nurturer. The group holds the hope that each woman feels about the possibility of its being a place where help can be got, where isolation can be broken and where pain can be released and tolerated. But the group often defends itself against these hopes and against the potential disappointment by the therapist. The women unconsciously feel that the therapist will not be able to handle all of the emotions in the group, that the therapist, another woman, will not be strong enough to contain the group. As a result we see many dynamics in the group to keep the therapist at bay, which are defences against this potential disappointment.

In the therapy group just as in individual therapy there are both the real relationships of the members and the therapist as well as transference relationships. The mother–daughter transference on to the therapist as well as on to group members is abundant. So many exchanges in the group trigger transference feelings and ensuing feelings of anger, disappointment, feeling misunderstood, etc. As the group relaxes more into itself and there are fewer defences against wanting from the therapist there may be struggles within the group for her attention. If she does give attention to one woman in the group it may trigger off in the other members their own longings, their own feelings of loss, their own feelings of not getting enough, their own fears of insatiability, their own competitive feelings towards other women. At the same time they may feel relief in seeing the therapist's ability to handle and help another group member. They feel that perhaps she can be there for them too. Because of both the transference feelings and all the other inevitable feelings with which each woman sits in a therapy group with other women, there are times when each woman feels surrounded by her feelings and perhaps encapsulated and therefore isolated within them. She wants contact with the other group members but, as we have seen at one level, this is not easy or straightforward. There are so many feelings filling the room – so much potential merger, boundarilessness and loss of self – that the transference seems to be bouncing off the circle created by the women. Feelings one woman may express of vulnerability, pain, anger or upset are so readily identified with by other group members. At times it may all seem too overwhelming and there are attempts to control the emerging feelings. Group members may cut off or interrupt a woman who is expressing her pain, for example, because of their own feelings of pain and their identification with the woman who is 'working'. The interruption is an attempt to quash the feelings, push them away and repress them in the same way as she does her own similar feelings. A group member's 'inability' to understand or tendency to be confused or perplexed or dismissive of another member's experience or feelings is another example of a defence against her own similar feelings. This dynamic parallels aspects of the mother–daughter relationship where, as we have discussed, mother pushes away aspects of her daughter's personality in the same way as she does with herself because her daughter's expression of certain needs and feelings stirs up ones which the mother herself must contain.

Another attempt at repression and containment is the phenomena of subgroupings within the group. Out of a fear of exposure and a desire for cover some women hold on to another member or several other members of the group. Anxieties from being in the group related to its open-endedness and the lack of boundaries that that may symbolize and fear of lack of control create a dynamic of subgrouping whereby a sense of containment and security are sought. The subgroupings provide interesting work for the group at two levels. The therapist is able to interpret the defensive aspects of this dynamic. The therapist in understanding and interpreting the dynamic provides a different form of containment and security. This allows group members to work on the second outcome of these subgroupings: the feelings of exclusion or inclusion of those outside or inside each subgroup (even if a woman is in another subgroup). These feelings of inclusion–exclusion open up the woman's past experiences of inclusion and exclusion in the family, at school, etc. Triangles of all sorts – mother, father, client; sister, mother, client, etc. – emerge and with them rich material to be worked on in the group.

As the women work on these various issues for themselves within the group there is another dynamic which flows through the group process. As we have seen, women are very unsympathetic to the little girl inside. They are always trying to push her away, to hide her. In a group where there are eight women and eight 'little girls', not only is it extremely reassuring to find out that every woman has a little girl inside, but it also makes this little girl less frightening. This, of course, is therapeutic in itself, but, perhaps more significant, as the women are able to be more sympathetic to other women's 'little girls inside' and the dilemma that other women feel about this part of themselves, so they can be more sympathetic to their own little girl inside. As each woman in the group experiences receiving

Outside In ... Inside Out

not only from the other members but also from the therapist, she becomes able to express her resentments, her upsets, her fears of abandonment. Yet the therapist, precisely because she is making herself available within the therapeutic context, can work through these issues and help the woman experience taking in the caring from all group members as well as herself. So being in an all-woman therapy group and having a therapist who is able to handle and provide nurturance to a lot of needy little girls and give to each of them is a very positive therapeutic experience.

Another theme that is woven into the group is that *all women want validation and they want it from women*. We described earlier how a little girl may turn to her father for things that her mother cannot give her. For perhaps the most difficult thing for a mother to give her daughter is validation, praise and a sense of self-worth, because she identifies with her daughter and lacks a sense of her own self-worth. So in general a woman comes to seek validation from men. But we suggest that the search for validation relates back to the difficulties in the mother–daughter relationship and that what women really want is validation from other women. In a women's therapy group a woman has a chance to change that experience through her relationship with the other women in the group.

Through the group, as women begin to see each other as multidimensional – to move away from that deeply held picture of woman as good or bad, needy or insatiable, all-powerful or all-withholding – so they can begin to apply that multidimensional texture to their own experience of themselves. As they listen to other women they begin to take each woman's experience seriously and thereby their own. Thus they begin to reverse deeply internalized feelings of low self-worth.

The experience of a women's therapy group is exciting, fascinating, deeply painful and can be radically transforming. One of the central dynamics throughout the process of the group is how the women develop a trust in the continuity of the group. As we recall at the beginning of the group, there is anxiety about 'will there be enough' and an unconscious preparation for loss; a sense of desperation about trying to get one's needs out and met within the group but with a sense of limited time, loss or disappointment which permeates the atmosphere. In the course of the group, this changes dramatically as the women gain a trust in the continuity of the group, of the continued nurturance and support which is available for them for as long as they need it.

Women in the group, then, come through a process of acceptance, discharge of pain, anger, upset and an understanding of unconscious patterns and psychological life. Each woman moves towards the process of separation from the group as her needs for the group change. Clearly, because of the psychology of women, a critical issue at a later stage of an analytic women's therapy group is that of separation and autonomy. The therapist and the other group members help to reverse the earlier experience with mother (and non-separation) and to move forward with other strong, separate, nurtured, loving women, still connected in 'healthy' contact. As we saw in individual therapy, this is a delicate process. In the group, one woman's proposed departure sparks off the other group members' complicated feelings related to abandonment, anger etc. The leaving of any one member, whether it be premature or appropriate, produces a rich situation for all involved, especially where the therapist is working to help each woman experience the sense of autonomy and separateness we have spoken of so much.

The therapist in a woman's therapy group is exposed to a tremendous amount of upset, distress, need, boundarilessness, self-hate, anger and competition, as well as love and nurturing, each week within the group. The therapist must be able to tolerate all of this with confidence. She must transmit to the group, through her behaviour and relatedness, that she will not be overwhelmed and taken over or annihilated by the group. As a woman herself many issues get raised. She may at times, especially towards the beginning of the group, fear that there is too much need and that she cannot possibly meet it. She at times feels pushed out of the group and must be able to tolerate this rejection, anger, criticism and negative transference which individual members of the group and the group as a whole direct towards her. She must be acutely aware of the *underlying* emotions expressed by the women, because so much that occurs on the surface is only the key to what the real emotional and therapeutic issues are. Perhaps, above all, the therapist must be keenly aware of her own boundaries. There is so much merger and boundarilessness in the group that she can, at times, feel swamped and taken over by all of these feelings, needs and 'little girls' in the group. The therapist must be able to remain separate and in her own boundaries in order to interpret for the group, work with the women, and be a safe and stable figure.

VI Somatic Symptoms and Phobias

We now discuss some psychological symptoms which are quite prevalent in women. Some of them specifically affect women and some affect both women and men. We will discuss phobias, obsessions, anorexia and compulsive eating, and how we understand these symptoms from a feminist perspective. We will refer to the general model that we have presented of women's ego development and describe these various symptoms as internal struggles related to that little-girl part of the woman and the structure of her ego. First, however, we want to make some general remarks about women's bodies and women's activity in the world. Women's social position means that the woman's sphere of influence is limited and that it is confined very much within her own home – if you like, within her own body. As we have observed, a woman's body is her primary asset in the world for with it she gains a man, a family, a home, a place in the world. A woman's body, therefore, is integral to her social position of wife and mother. At the same time, as we know, certain aspects of a woman's life inevitably cause conflict which it may be impossible to express. The distress a woman feels, the conflicts she experiences, the taboos against her longings often show themselves, not surprisingly, in women's terrain: her body. A woman may unconsciously express her distress through her body – a somatic symptom; or her body may react in a terrorized way to a particular object or event – a phobia.

When a person has a phobic reaction to a particular object or event they are in the grip of a terrorizing and fearful experience in which they feel utterly helpless. A woman who has a phobic reaction to riding in a lift, for example, is terrified at the idea of having to enter one and be in the lift. She cannot imagine that she will survive the experience. The idea of having to go through with it paralyses her and feels absolutely impossible.

There are women with multiple phobias, women with just one type of phobia, women who have shifting phobias or who have phobias that only come out under acute circumstances. There are women who have their phobias under reasonable control or management – for example they do not like birds but they can avoid them in a fairly straightforward way. We discuss the woman who feels incapacitated by a phobia, whose fear is with her on a continual basis because this is what we have heard most about in our practice.

Phobias can be understood as defence structures within the split ego. We have described the way in which bad feelings are often split off and repressed within the ego. This phenomenon combines with another mechanism of the psyche – that of projection. Projection is the process of unconsciously placing a part of oneself or feelings one might have outside and on to another person or object. For example, Alison is angry but is fearful of her anger so she projects this anger on to John and thinks and experiences John as angry. In other words she sees her own angry feelings in him. Phobias can be understood by grasping these two concepts – splitting and projection. What happens with a phobia is that a woman attempts (unconsciously) to cope with the bad internal feelings by projecting them outside of herself on to something else. The feelings are thrown out into the world and then the badness and danger is experienced as coming from the outside. The bad feelings are discharged and placed outside of the person rather than repressed; the train, spider, plane, etc. takes on all of the badness. If all the 'badness' is contained in an outside object, then the woman has a certain distance, so that she does not feel that she, a fleeting security, has the 'badness' inside her. For the phobic woman the bad feelings about herself are so intolerable that she cannot come near them.

Initially the phobia may, in a sense, serve its function – of keeping the bad feelings at bay. However, as the symptom persists the woman may come to feel ashamed and upset about this disability and so the bad feelings and upset catch up with her. The phobia surrounds her and she cannot escape. There are several points about phobic experiences that are essential for the therapist to understand. One is that the woman is in fact out of control of the terrifying feelings; at any moment they could completely overwhelm her and reduce her to a state of panic. In fact many women describe phobias as 'panic attacks'. For some women the phobias may be successfully compartmentalized in such a way that only certain situations bring on the panic, such as travelling by Tube or crossing bridges. These women may have no real experience of themselves as being in psychological distress. They may feel they have a peculiar reaction to the specific activity. For other women the experience of distress may be more acute. They may continuously experience this panic and potential terror of being taken over by the badness and disintegrated feelings. This is often the fear behind the phobia. The woman fears that she will be stranded in terror or that she will fall apart.

The onset of a phobia is usually unexpected. The individual so affected often has had no previous experience of being in psychological distress. Generally the onset of a phobia is triggered by one or a series of bad situations in the external world, such as the loss of a loved one, or the loss of critical elements in one's emotional security. This loss then creates a situation of internal collapse. The woman may have been relying heavily on her relationships in order to feel any sense of security. A significant loss, then, breaks the illusory security of her well-being and throws her into a state of being with herself and her 'bad' internal object relations.

Let us take a look at the ego structure of such a woman to see why she comes to be susceptible to phobias. The woman has not experienced suffi- cient, consistent nurturing so she has not embodied a solid sense of self. In her early development she has not received adequate care, attention and containment so that upsetting feelings and experiences could be gone through and tolerated. Along the continuum of inconsistency in relating that we have seen in women's psychological development (see Chapters 1 and 2) the phobic woman has experienced extreme inconsistency in early relating. She has not embodied sufficient security and love, so her ego structure is precarious. She does not have the capacity to reassure herself and she is flooded by bad feelings. These feelings then get packaged and projected on to an outside object in the attempt to maintain a sense of internal safety.

When we look to the actual meaning of specific phobias it is very im- portant to explore the range of meanings for the woman concerned. For example, when a woman has a transportation phobia, what is it that she is terrified of? Is it moving from one place to another? Is it being in transit? Is it being trapped? Is it being suspended on a bridge with no platform? Transportation phobias are very common among women. If a woman cannot go from point A to point B, it may be that she cannot leave point A – that she cannot leave the security, however unsatisfactory, that she has found at point A. Or it may be that she cannot get to point B because she does not feel sufficiently secure within herself to cope with a new situation; she does not have the expectation that a new situation will have anything good to offer because her previous experiences have been so unsatisfactory. For many phobic women their lack of internal continuity means that in moving from point A to point B they risk losing themselves. One fear that we have heard expressed many times is that it is not reaching point B or leaving point A that is the difficulty, it is being trapped in a situation (such as the Tube or a plane) that makes the woman feel she has no self, that she will go 'mad'. Symbolically being in the plane represents her lack of control and her vulnerability. She is in one sense alone and trapped with her depleted self. She cannot escape and at the same time she has to give up control to another. The plane may represent the badness that entraps her.

The existence of psychological false boundaries in the psychology of women can be most dramatically seen in the symptom of agoraphobia. Ninety-five per cent of agoraphobics are women [1]. What we have to understand is why a particular woman is frightened to leave her house. What does she fear? Is it leaving the home base? Is the home the only safe place for her? Is it arriving somewhere else? Is it being with other people? Is it being alone in the world? There is a different meaning for each of these things that will relate to the particular woman's ego development and her defence structure. For the agoraphobic woman the boundaries of her own home substitute for her psychological boundaries. A woman may feel that if she steps outside of these boundaries she will lose herself. Many women who are agoraphobic also have allied feelings of claustrophobia. The false external boundaries not only serve to contain and 'protect' her; at the same time they also trap her. Once again the woman suffers by being surrounded by and unable to get away from her distress. Her symptom of agoraphobia is a representation of the psychic prison she is in.

Another symptom which illustrates the somaticization of psychological states for women is that of vaginismus. Vaginismus is the involuntary tightening of the vaginal muscles which then prevents penetration. One way to understand vaginismus is to see it as the woman's fear of being taken over, of being invaded and of losing herself. She has a shaky sense of her psychological boundaries and so her physical body is the only boundary that she 'knows'. (This operates, of course, on an unconscious level.) Intercourse then is the penetration of her boundaries, an invasion of herself. Vaginismus is a physical expression of the creation of false boundaries in an attempt to maintain or erect a sense of self. The rigid boundaries (expressed through the closing of the vagina) prevent merger because the merger may bring with it a fear of disintegration and loss of self in the other.

Some women become phobic after marriage [2] when they have left their parents' home and are making a life with a partner of their choice. On the face of it marriage provides a woman with the possibility of a consistent loving partner. Marriage, particularly the myth surrounding romantic love, holds out the possibility that at last one will be understood, met and cherished. The woman is brought up to believe that she will find her happiness in marriage. Of course, many women and men do find their marriages fulfilling, but for a woman whose ego structure is unintegrated, marriage may jar psychically for it may dispel, at an unconscious level, the fantasy that she can find the acceptance in her partner that she had been searching for from her mother (see next chapter). Alternatively, a loving relationship may bring up all the hidden feelings of rage, loss and hurt because of the disappointment with her original love object. The new intimacy brings up these feelings and exposes the hidden little-girl. If the woman cannot contain these feelings they become somaticized. Marriage can also trigger off the unconscious desire for merger with the partner. The false boundaries dissolve and the woman 'merges' with her partner. The phobia then simultaneously represents her need to be cared for – she cannot travel, go out and so on – and at the same time keeps her apart in psychological isolation. Her attachment in marriage may highlight her needs for the other, and so actual, external separation becomes impossible. The phobia is a symptom of the woman's fear of separation.

Obsessional Anxieties

In our clinical practice we often encounter the symptom of obsessional anxieties. For example, a woman leaving her house may have to return to check that she has turned off the gas, locked the door, etc. ten times before feeling safe in her departure. A woman may need to scrub her pots an increasing number of times in order to feel satisfied that they are clean and bear no traces of dirt.

A psychological developmental explanation for these obsessions can be found if we remind ourselves of how in early ego development the infant takes into herself the difficult experiences and tries to change them around by having a different relationship to her internal objects. In the case of obsessions this same psychic phenomenon goes on. For example, a woman feels upset about a particular situation. Unconsciously (or perhaps consciously) she feels out of control. She gets obsessed with thinking about the situation. She mulls it over in her mind and tries to make it work out in a different way. She works it over and over, listing it, thinking about it, trying to change it, getting caught up in trying to transform her experience because she does not feel that she has any control over changing it in reality. She attempts to do all the changing inside her head. This becomes a very internal experience. As the woman becomes increasingly caught up with trying to manipulate the situation internally she avoids the painful feelings which arose from the initial reality of the difficult situation. In therapy we want to help the woman to explore the painful experience that she is trying to transform internally and get away from. We sit with her in it. The therapist's ability to contain the upset lessens the woman's psychic fear.

Anorexia and Compulsive Eating

We now discuss anorexia and compulsive eating and focus on the meanings of these symptoms at an object-relational developmental level for women [3]. Of the two expressions anorexia is a much more serious psychological distress symptom than compulsive eating, although there are aspects of compulsive eating, particularly in the case of extremely obese compulsive eaters, that express on a continuum the same kind of distress symptoms as anorexia. In anorexia we see the same attempt on the part of the individual woman to split off the painful and bad experiences she has had and is currently having. The woman cannot tolerate her feelings. She experiences her emotional life as an attack on herself, and she attempts to control it so that she will not be devoured by her emotions. She tries to gain control over her body and mind by creating an altogether new person inside herself. In other words she rejects her needy, hungry, yearning self and tries to submit this to extreme rules and regulations and in so doing create a persona for herself that she finds acceptable. So she will adopt an extreme regime of diet and exercise where, for example, she may have to run several miles each day or engage in strenuous exercise in order to sit down for half an hour. In turn, submission to the exercises creates a boundary between the woman and her needs. She feels a strength but it is a false sense of strength as it is dependent on her vigilance and is in danger of collapse at any time. Further, this new defence isolates the woman from the possibility of knowing what her real needs might be and from tapping into the real strength that comes from being able to accept one's needs. She must instead deny herself, and in the denying create a person who she can admire, *a person who has no needs and appetites*.

The anorectic woman relates to her body as she relates to her emotional life. At certain points in her life her body has shown itself to be outside her control by producing periods, breasts, hips. Her body insists, 'Here I am. I'm changing. You can't control me' and she feels 'Yes, I will control you, I will transform you. I will not have breasts, I will not have hips and I will not have periods. I will not be a woman. I will not be like you, mother. I will not reproduce your life and I will not take in your food. I will not take you inside of me, I will make myself into something else, something other than you.' The paradox, of course, is that in trying to gain control over her body and emotions and gain a sense of self-worth, she institutes rules which then she holds on to and keeps to religiously, at the same time depriving herself of food and thereby causing herself great harm. (Anorexia is treated so seriously precisely because it can lead to death.) In trying to split off the 'bad' part of herself and in trying to give herself something good to hold on to, i.e. the rules and regulations, the anorectic may be killing herself. As she tries to control the feeling part of her, she is destroying her body and so tragically and paradoxically in her struggles for control over herself she may actually lose herself.

Anorectics do intermittently rebel against their self-imposed strictures. This often is expressed by bingeing. Unfortunately they cannot hold on to the food that they allow themselves; they have to purge themselves of it, by laxatives or by vomiting. Yet the part of the anorectic woman which initiated the binge was attempting to get nurturance, food, love and life. It is this part that is struggling towards life that the therapist can catch hold of and work with.

Just as other defences are used to cover the needy little-girl inside, so too is compulsive eating a protective mechanism. The compulsive eating behaviour contains for the woman a fear that nobody will give to her; that she cannot get what she wants; that she has not had enough; that she will be insatiable. It symbolizes the woman's struggle to get. It is an attempt to give to herself. Unlike the anorectic, the compulsive eater is attempting to nurture herself, however painfully she goes about it. There is at some unconscious level an acknowledgement of need, yet at the same time when a woman is eating compulsively she is pushing down that need, at an emotional level. She is hiding her little-girl and at the same time her fat lets the world know that she does have needs. Her fat simultaneously creates an outside physical boundary covering the little-girl.

For a compulsive eater, at an unconscious level being thin and giving up the fat represents starving – starving emotionally, having needs exposed and unmet. Her needs will be visible, her deprivation will be uncovered. It is as if, without the protective cover of her fat, her neediness will scream out.

When working clinically it is most important to understand the symbolic meanings of body states for compulsive eaters and for anorectics. It is also important to realize that both of these expressions of eating disorders can be full-time obsessions, and as we have pointed out, obsessions are distractions from the real underlying feelings of distress. In anorexia and compulsive eating what we see are women trying to change the shapes of their lives by trying to change the shapes of their bodies.

Dynamics between Couples and Implications for Couple Counselling

In our experience with couple counselling, the couple usually seeks a therapist when there is severe crisis within the relationship which the couple cannot work through together. The couple has been suffering together for quite some time, unable to get out of the knots and tangles they feel themselves to be in. Communication between the two people has broken down considerably and each person may feel misunderstood by the other. It may feel as though the feelings between them which were once loving and sweet have gone sour; they now feel upset, anger and bad feelings between them. They cannot rely on the good feelings between them.

What we want to focus on are the underlying dynamics of how two people, who are sexually involved, achieve intimacy and closeness with one another and some of the reasons for difficulties within intimate relationships [1]. In discussing this issue we think there are more parallels than differences between heterosexual and lesbian relationships; so first we will be describing the overall theme of intimacy and separateness, and then we will point more specifically to the different dynamics in heterosexual and lesbian relationships.

The fabric of intimacy is woven by three elements; boundaries, dependency and separateness. When a relationship begins it may appear to be an easy process of opening oneself up, of being eager to be close to another person. At the same time each person comes to the relationship with protections and boundaries because emotional trust has not yet been built. The caring, gentleness, understanding, excitement, warmth and concern of each partner builds trust between the two. As the trust develops in a relationship the distance between the two people begins to disappear and the intimacy reaches a new depth. Achieving a truly satisfactory and 'healthy' relationship, however, is no easy feat, for people bring with them all the complexities of their psychologies; protections, feelings of fear, insecurity, anger, difficulties in receiving and giving love, together with issues of sexuality, making for a very complicated situation. Each person also

91

Outside In . . . Inside Out

brings a range of expectations, even if unconscious, about who this person is going to be for them.

Dependency is a central issue in all relationships and is especially critical in intimate sexual relationships. At the same time as intimacy grows in a relationship, the people are developing emotional dependency on one another. There is a recognition of caring, of a connection, of emotional nurturance given to each other that is both needed and wanted. Commitment and a sense of being responsible towards the other person are facets of this dependency.

What we tend to find is that one person within the relationship, usually the woman, carries the insecurity and the feelings of dependency for both partners. Now if one person feels insecure and very dependent, then the other person within the couple can feel quite secure, confident that they are not going to be abandoned. If one person holds tightly, the other can feel secure. Although both men and women have difficulties with their dependency needs, it may be that the woman appears to be the dependent partner because of the dynamics of sexual politics, i.e. the woman needs the man more than the man appears to need the woman. Let us recapitulate on why this dynamic of the woman carrying the dependency needs come about. Men go from their mothers to another woman; by and large they have the security of a woman in their lives. They can depend on the relationship. This sense of having someone there and the security it produces allows the man in a relationship to feel more separate, to partake in activities outside the relationship confident that the woman is there waiting for him. For the woman, however, both previous experience and her psychology produce an anxiety that she will lose the person that she loves, that she will have to curb her dependency needs, not expect to be looked after emotionally, that she will be pushed away. This has happened with mother. Father also comes and goes. So for the woman there is no such confidence that this needed and loved person will be there securely for her. Because her emotional dependency needs are cut short and because she cannot then express them directly she may exhibit a certain kind of clinginess in an intimate relationship.

When we explore these themes within a couple-counselling situation what we usually find is that the man is just as dependent upon the woman as she is on him. When the woman exhibits some autonomy and separateness, suddenly the man's insecurity and fear of losing the person upon whom he is dependent become apparent. His emotional dependency is unveiled.

People have an ability to seek each other out – to find someone with whom they 'fit' psychologically. This is part of the attraction and has both positive and problematic aspects. Very often in counselling a couple, we can see that one person keeps tight boundaries while the other seems to be searching and reaching out for contact with the other. In courtship this may be part of the challenge but in the ongoing life of the couple it can cause frustration. It is as if the boundaries have to be kept by someone. This unfortunate fit, caused by the fear of intimacy, leads to a bad spiral in which the more the one person keeps up the boundaries, the more the other feels forced to push through them. However, the more the person pushes in an attempt to make contact and be close, the more the other puts up a firm wall as a defence, because of the fear of intimacy. This dynamic confirms the fears of both people. The person who is keeping up the boundaries fears being taken over, controlled and suffocated by his or her partner, and the experience of the partner trying to push through the boundaries seems to confirm this fear. The lover's attempts to get close are experienced as forceful intrusions or demands. The person who tries to make the contact fears that the partner will reject him or her and this fear is also confirmed, as are his or her feelings about being too 'hungry' and demanding. When a woman is the partner actively seeking contact, her fear of having an unending well of need inside her, of being insatiable, also seems confirmed, because the more she is kept at a distance and not given to, the more her need is felt and the greater it seems.

For many couples this dynamic remains consistent with each partner staying in his or her respective position. However, in certain couples this dynamic may shift back and forth rather like in the cha-cha dance where when one partner goes forward, the other goes back, and then the reverse. The shift occurs when the partner who was carrying the dependency, holding on, trying to push through the boundaries, stops and steps back. The person may step back as a result of frustration, anger, disappointment or a sense of hopelessness about being able to reach the other partner. As the one retreats, so to speak, there is now a new space between the two – a space that previously was filled with the yearnings of the one partner. In this new space several things occur. First, the partner 'behind the wall' experiences the absence of what was felt to be pressure. But, more important, what is felt is the *absence* of the other's attention. The solidness of the wall may dissolve slightly as the person begins to experience his or her own need for the other. He or she may now feel abandoned, frightened of losing the other and more aware of dependent feelings. This cha-cha can be very upsetting and frustrating for both partners because the closeness which they may both seek is so hard to achieve.

Now if we were to describe the healthy model of an adult couple we might say that each of the people comes to the relationship with a secure, defined and generally positive sense of self, together with the ability to receive and give love. Because of this secure sense of self each person also brings into the relationship the ability to have the other be separate. One is not looking to the other to fill the emptiness inside. Rather, two 'whole' people come together, share love and intimacy, and merge emotionally, physically and sexually without fear. What this means is, ideally again, that each person would have the ability to open up, merge and to separate without the fear of loss of self or loss of the other person. This model of the 'healthy' couple is one that is not very familiar to any of us; few couples have achieved this state. What we find in couples who are having difficulties and therefore seeking counselling is a more diffused sense of boundaries, a lack of secure sense of self; each is seeking in the other the longed-for loving person they want, or the longed-for self that she or he cannot be.

The dynamic of projection is very apparent in couples. People see qualities in their loved ones that they admire and desire for themselves. Many couples appear from the outside to have quite opposite characteristics in their personalities. Again, this is part of the attraction, challenge and excitement of a relationship. Each person wishes to expand and express through the couple hidden aspects of their personality. However, this dynamic of projection can also cause problems because of the blurring of boundaries that sexual intimacy may produce. Each partner may see an unwanted aspect of self in the other and be judgemental towards their partner. A woman uneasy with her own vulnerability may defend against seeing it in her partner. A man uncomfortable in his social relationship may see *his* unease in his partner in social situations.

As well as this dynamic of projection, there is a tendency in couples to transmit their hopes, desires, expectations and anxieties to each other. One partner may transmit his or her views on a particular topic or experience to the other and presume that they are mirrored by the partner. Knots can arise from hidden expectations and the difficulty each person may have in exposing their differences or accepting those of their partner.

There is a sensitivity that seems to go along with sexual relationships that is not found in friendships. It is as if the boundaries of disappointment, anger and hurt can be crossed far more easily. Within friendships people are often able to contain their feelings more 'appropriately'. Within sexual relationships the boundaries which have been crossed physically seem to leave open paths and avenues which the emotions traverse. Unspoken demands, assumptions and expectations are part and parcel of the sexual relationship, so that feelings of disappointment or anger are easily triggered, often without the lover's knowledge or awareness. In couple counselling the therapist is trying to help the couple to dissect and uncover these expectations and assumptions so that a clearer communication can take place between the two people.

In addition, within heterosexual relationships both the man and the woman have all kinds of assumptions and expectations as a result of sex-role stereotyping in patriarchal society. Some of these are obvious but that does not mean that they are not deeply embedded in all of our psychologies. So for example the meaning of a woman's desire for a 'strong' man or the meaning of a man's desire for a 'gentle, caring' woman will find expression in the relationship. The feminist therapist will bear these in mind and use them as an important part of the work that goes on in trying to help a couple achieve a more equal, interdependent intimacy.

The issue of woman's separateness may present itself as a problem in contemporary relationships (since the changes in consciousness brought about by the Women's Liberation Movement). Both women and men see women's separateness as something to be feared (see Chapter 2), and so couples may unconsciously collude to keep the woman restrained and not separate from the relationship. Her autonomy produces difficulty. As we have discussed, both men's and women's first dependent and primary relationship was with a woman and we all carry a sore spot of fear of abandonment and loss of a woman. Women's separateness in a couple arouses these deeply held feelings. In the counselling context once a woman's neediness is no longer seen to be the major problem (which it is so often thought to be at first), we then see many of the feelings that men have about their own inadequacy in nurturing and in relating intimately. We may find that the man gets very frightened when he sees that the woman is upset or angry with him, and he may try to protect himself and defend against his own vulnerability. He may feel like a little boy being told he had disappointed, angered or upset his mother. He may not know how to give or what to give. Often men's vulnerability and feelings of inadequacy are converted into anger. The anger operates as a defence to cover up the vulnerable feelings and protect them from exposure. This illustrates a common 'fit' in heterosexual couples. The defensive anger of the man entwines with the woman's fear of anger and her own feelings of unentitlement. The anger may discourage her from pursuing what she feels she wants. She retreats.

Both people in a heterosexual couple-counselling situation have much to gain, but it is a very difficult struggle. Our overall goal would be for both people within the relationship to recognize their love and need for one another, at the same time as being able to achieve psychological separateness and autonomy.

Lesbian Relationships

Lesbian relationships raise the same issues that we have discussed above in relation to intimacy, boundaries, dependency and separateness, but perhaps in a different way. First of all and most important, the lesbian relationship is set within a context in which there is a tension about being in a relationship that is not accepted within the culture at large. So, although many of the emotional dynamics may be similar to heterosexual relationships, the context within which the relationship exists is different. Laws of patriarchal culture allow for heterosexual love and outlaw sexual love between women. For a lesbian couple there is the constant threat of the culture coming into the context of the relationship and bringing with it condemnation, punishment, attacks of shame and guilt. There is, even in the early 1980s, little support for lesbian couples apart from within the lesbian community. It is therefore very difficult for lesbians to expose the problems within their relationship because the general response of people is still to see the problem as having to do with the choice of sexuality, i.e. the problem is seen as the sexual choice and not the emotional dynamics between the women in the couple. Of course, this is never seen to be the case with heterosexual couples – no one ever thinks that maybe having chosen to be heterosexual is what is causing the problems.

The issue of boundaries and closeness have a different edge when there are two women involved. In our experience many mother–daughter dynamics cross from one partner to the other within lesbian relationships. Issues arise such as that of the woman attempting to define herself as separate from another woman; trying to experience herself as different from her lover; expressing, giving and receiving love from another woman; and the inevitable projections and identifications that occur between two women who are close. Perhaps the fear of merger with *another woman* heightens the unconscious memory of the earlier relationship with mother.

In lesbian relationships there are two 'little girls' as well as two potential 'mothers' in the situation. Each woman brings to the relationship her little girl inside, yearning to be loved, cared for, accepted and validated by another woman. But, as we have seen, the little girl inside also brings feelings of tremendous neediness, anxieties about rejection, abandonment, disappointment, as well as feelings of anger. Lesbian relationships contain the possibility of nurture and love shared between two women. Both women have been raised to 'mother' – to care for others, to have emotional antennae etc. There may be a reciprocal nurturance.

In the couple counselling situation we see the difficulties the women are

96

having in coping with each other's little girl inside. As we know, it is a problem for women to accept that part of themselves and so women defend against the exposure of the little girl inside. This is no less true in lesbian relationships, where often both women are simultaneously attempting to curb their own neediness at the same time as the needs of their lover stimulate their own. There may be an identification on the part of the two little girls inside that can be difficult to accept and handle. A feminist therapist tries to help the two women to express and accept their own emotional needs as well as those of their lovers' so that the appropriate caring can take place. Other dynamics that we see in our practice in lesbian relationships are the themes that are present in women's relationships in general: envy, competition, betrayal, anger etc. In a lesbian couple there are two women with women's psychology and so many of the aspects we have discussed in Chapter 5 are present in the relationship. The sexual relationship adds, often, to the intensity of these feelings.

We find that the dynamics of intimacy, merger and separateness are similar in heterosexual couples and lesbian couples. The cha-cha dynamic we have discussed applies equally to lesbian couples.

Above all, feminist therapists must be aware of the social and political difficulties facing lesbian couples. Only with that awareness on the part of the therapist can a lesbian couple seek couple counselling without the threat of their choice of partner being placed in the forefront of their problems.

Achieving 'healthy' intimate relationships – relationships where both people are equal and interdependent – has fundamental implications for the structure of the family unit. Heterosexual relationships at present are built on inequalities between men and women. In Chapter 8 we shall move on to speculate about the future were such dramatic changes to take place in the psychology of women and men.

VIII   Looking Forward

It will be clear now, from the kind of theory we have been presenting, that we see psychic structure as fluid. It is constructed under particular conditions in a particular way; and the present psychic structure of women derives from current child-rearing arrangements in which women bring up children in patriarchal society. Our position has been that our psychic structure is based on a translation of culture, of material conditions, of actual personal relationships, the power relationships within the family and the psychodynamics of those relationships. Any psychic structural change at a fundamental and a mass level will only arise from a change in the material conditions in which children are raised, and from a change in the social position of women. In this chapter we want to discuss both the changing position of women and how to change individual psychology, as both these issues play an important part in breaking the cycle of damaging self-hatred that operates between generations of women.

The process of uncovering the ways in which femininity is reproduced has gone hand in hand with the activities and the vision of the Women's Liberation Movement. The Women's Liberation Movement has opened the way to seeing how the tragic cycle of socialization from mothers to daughters can begin to be broken. New forms of child-rearing and family relationships are emerging. It has understood that the way 'women are made' [1] is inextricably bound up with women's social position. Adrienne Rich writes, in *Of Woman Born*: 'A woman who has respect and affection for her own body, who does not view it as unclean or as a sex object, will wordlessly transmit to her daughter that a woman's body is a good and healthy place to live. A woman who feels pride in being female will not visit her self-depreciation upon her female children.' This social position, and hence women's experience of self, will take several generations to change. In general terms we argue for the equal involvement of both parents in the raising of children and for the presence of both sexes in the early life of children (so that we will see men child-minders, nursery-school teachers etc). If there is no move towards balance between the sexes, the

98

general position of women (even if individually some women may not experience the dreadful feelings of unworthiness and self-doubt) and the reproduction of a feminine psychic structure such as we have described will not change.

The kind of structural psychological shifts that we think necessary cannot be sufficiently implemented in one generation. Women and men currently carry within them deep feelings of misogyny and unconscious sexism. Even with changes in child-rearing arrangements, these influences will have their impact on the first generation raised by two parents, for, as we have seen, the progress of psychological development involves the embodying of the psychologies of our caretakers in early life. This is not to be discouraging but rather to stress the seriousness of the project at hand, and emphasize the necessity of the long-term approach to such structural changes.

The changes in the family and in child-rearing practices will have an effect in many ways. With fathers involved in the raising of children, the psychology of the father himself will alter. Men are going to have to change radically and develop areas of themselves that are as yet unexplored. They will have to experience the feelings of inadequacy, of anxiety, and vulnerability that accompany the necessary opening up to, taking in and learning about the skills of nurturance. They will expose their vulnerability as they develop and express that part of themselves. Men learning to become nurturers and fathers will, of course, dramatically affect the psyches of the children who are being raised. For a little boy who is being raised by a father as well as a mother, several things will be vastly different from traditional mothering. First, he will be able to develop a sense of male gender by identifying with his father. He will be developing a secure sense of himself as male that does not depend on establishing defensive differences with women. (Currently the boy develops his sense of self in opposition to his mother, who is female and 'other' [2].) The psychology that the boy embodies will contain the psychologies of both his parents. His positive experiences will relate to both sexes as will his negative ones. He will experience the power of nurturance and boundary-drawing, restrictions, etc. from a man as well as a woman. He will experience strong feelings of love as well as anger and hate towards both a man and a woman. These changes will contribute to the transformation of the misogynist nature of a masculine psychology.

Boys being raised by a father as well as a mother will be allowed and encouraged to develop their own nurturing abilities in previously unknown ways. By seeing his father, a male, engaged in a variety of nurturing and domestic activities, the boy will come to feel that this too is his world. This impact will be felt in the boy's relationships inside and outside the family. He will bring a nurturing self both to his relationships with his peers and his intimate sexual relationships.

A little girl being raised by both a father and a mother will also experience radical shifts in her psychology. First of all she will have an early close relationship with father. Fathers, and hence men, will lose their mystique – they will no longer be seen as remote and unknowable. Emotionality will become associated with both sexes, and the girl will grow into a woman who has a reasonable expectation of receiving emotional nurturance and emotional consistency from men.

If there are two parenting adults there will be dramatic changes in a girl's psychic structural development during the period of infantile dependency. We have discussed how the nurturance that girls receive in this period is at present extremely staccato and contains a push–pull dynamic leading to a fundamental feeling of insecurity and lack of self-esteem. If the period of infantile dependency is no longer the responsibility of one parent who is both over- and undervalued in her role as mother, and is herself a needy person, but is instead an experience shared by two confident, mature adults, then what the infant embodies from them in the process of becoming a person will be very different. This is what we mean when we say that these changes will take several generations to come into effect. The joyful nature of parenting shared in this way will be communicated and transmitted to the baby. Nurturance, confidence, pleasure and wholesome engagement will be a part of the relating. The baby's contentment and security will be communicated back to the parents, contributing towards their confidence and pleasure in the parenting process. For the first generation of children raised by both parents, the mother's psychology and the father's psychology that the girl child embodies will reflect aspects of a mother's negative self-image and neediness and of a father's fear and misogyny. Mother may feel less needy because she does not have sole responsibility for her child and she can feel the support of her partner, but this will not dispense with all of her feelings of deprivation and confusions about her entitlements. Similarly, the first generation of fathers who nurture will feel somewhat hesitant and nervous in their new role. They may transmit feelings of inadequacy and resentment to their children.

But let us move on several generations and project the new psychic structure for girls. If two parents are rearing children together we can assume that it would be easier for them to cope with a child's distress. At present, we have seen, a baby girl's distress triggers off in the mother a special identification with her own distress and reflects her fears of bad mothering; her comforting of her daughter's pain is tinged with the desire to push it away. Two parents, neither of whom over-identifies with the daughter, may enable the infant girl to tolerate painful experiences and so come to feel she can survive them, and also to feel that her feelings are not so dangerous. At a psychic structural level, the child's negative experiences will not all be centred around mother. So just as the girl (and the boy) embody two parents in the positive nurturing experiences which promote ego development, so too will the negative and difficult experiences be associated with two parents, two people with different genders. All badness will no longer derive from experiences of disappointment with women. The implications for the eradication of misogyny are profound in terms of the girl's psychology. She will not have the deeply embedded experience that at bottom what mother is, what she herself is and can be, what all women are, is at once all good and all bad [2].

A change in the deep psychic distrust of women will be paralleled with a change in how girls see women and men in their sex roles. Because both men and women would be involved in the domestic labour that is so much a part of daily life, little girls, who would still be learning domestic skills, would not come to see it as second-class work; it would be seen, rightly we believe, as a necessary part of life, neither falsely under- or overvalued. The sense of sexual inequality presently attached to the division of labour would change and create a shift in a woman's self-esteem. She would come to feel that she is a participant in human activity rather than someone whose work is both invisible and misvalued.

The change from women's sole responsibility for the household and child-rearing would have to be accompanied by a change in employment possibilities for women and men and a restructuring of the labour process. This in turn would have an impact on a girl's experience of womanhood. A child growing up in an environment where both parents have commitments at work and outside the family will have a very different sense of who both women and men are and what to expect of them.

The kinds of changes we are advocating will not occur without tremendous upheaval at both a psychological and a social level. For example, it is unrealistic to think that a woman could easily relinquish the power and impact she does currently have in the family: the organization of the household and the control and socialization of the children. Even where an important outside interest engages her, she feels a loss of self-definition and social standing by moving outside the image of femininity that she carries inside of her. As a woman gives up some of her control she may experience a sense of loss and disorientation; she may feel embarrassed and humiliated at her partner taking on aspects of a social role previously deemed correct for her, incorrect for him. Similarly, men who have the best intentions and a commitment to a restructuring of sexual politics may feel awkward and out of place, inadequate and clumsy in their new role as nurturers and equal partners.

The possibility of girls and boys being raised by both parents, then, will have a profound impact on the psychological profile of femininity and masculinity. Girls and boys will have the chance to develop the nurturing aspects of themselves – not from a position of neediness, as is now so often the case with girls, or defensiveness, which is how men under pressure develop nurturing qualities – but from a position of having received an unambiguous, wholesome, well-nurtured childhood.

Girls and boys both will come to psychological separation from their parents from a position of strength and a sense of wholeness. At present girls rarely achieve psychological separation and boys' psychological separation is imbued with a deep defensiveness. The melting of false boundaries in both sexes will occur with an authentic experience of selfhood. Girls' and boys' psychic structures will reflect the embodiment of positive and negative experiences with both women and men. Mother will no longer represent the person who has the power to give all or to withhold all. Intimacy will include rich experiences with father, and mother's image will necessarily be modified.

The new ways of relating these changes will bring about are as yet unforeseeable. We can guess at the outlines but only barely glimpse the details of the wealth of possibilities in friendship, sexual relations and parenting. In friendship all women will perhaps be able to achieve what has begun to be achieved as a result of the work of the Women's Liberation Movement: honest, loving relationships built not on fear or betrayal, competition, envy, or solidarity in opposition to men etc., but relationships built on sharing, contact between equals and a support for autonomy. In friendships between women and men we can look forward to an equal exchange of emotionality and strength. Friendships between men will allow for a disclosure of self and the knowledge that men can nurture and support each other.

In heterosexual relations we can foresee a coming together of a woman and a man on the basis of two separate and autonomous people seeking intimacy, neither of whom fears women, and in the woman's case freed of the mystery that surrounds 'having a man'. With psychological separateness and economic independence, women and men can relate to one another on the basis of equal exchange, rather than that of the man providing financial security and the woman emotional nurturance. It will be possible for both partners to recognize their dependency on each other, to share together their emotional world and abandon the cha-cha dynamic. The respect a woman will come to feel for herself means that she will not need to seek confirmation of her self-worth through a man's approval. Similarly, a man's secure knowledge of his own boundaries will not force him to present himself in opposition to a woman. In lesbian relationships we can look forward to two strong, loved women giving to each other; not from neediness or over-identification and with resentment, but on the basis of appreciation in loving a woman who is like oneself but also separate. Within homosexual relations we can speculate that certain painful aspects of self-hatred and animosity towards women will dissolve, so that the love men feel for each other can flourish.

The kinds of changes we are projecting are a glimpse down one particular pathway. The recontextualizing of our lives, the struggle against patriarchy, will require social upheaval spread over many generations. In our time there has been a profound questioning of the nuclear family, which has been accompanied by an acceleration in divorce, single parenting, communal living and cooperative communities. Some of these divergences and new ways of parenting have been pursued intentionally [3] while some are still practised with the image and desire of the nuclear family in mind. It will be several generations before the effects of the new parenting arrangements on psychic structure can be assessed, and this will require a sensitive understanding of the many diverse paths that people are now exploring.

Appendix: The Roots of Feminist Psychotherapy in Psychoanalysis

Psychoanalysis has evolved from a treatment of mental distress to a developmental theory of the workings of the human psyche. In this appendix we want to give a brief overview of the work of Freud and the post-Freudians, and the object relations theorists, in order to show how our own feminist view of women's psychology has evolved.

Freud

The nature of female sexuality has been hotly debated within psychoanalytic circles ever since Freud focused attention on the importance of sexuality in everyday life and in the history of civilization. At the turn of the century Freud's discovery of an infantile and childhood sexuality was a radical departure from the Victorian denial of its existence. Psychoanalysis has evolved from a treatment for mental distress to a developmental theory of the workings of the human psyche. At the very centre of his theory of psychological development Freud placed libido – the human being's struggle to come to terms with her or his sexuality and life energy. Freud asserted that the force of libido could be seen in every aspect of human activity as people repressed and sublimated it. Libido always sought satisfaction, and it was the harnessing of libidinous desires that led to the creation of civilization as we know it. In psychic terms, mental functioning depended on the individual's capacity to repress and express her or his sexuality according to the cultural norm.

Freud gathered the data for his theory through the process of psychoanalysis. By analysing distress symptoms and exploring the unconscious material of his patients through free association, slips of the tongue and dreams, he built a theory of psychological development. Freud saw mental life going through a series of stages – oral, anal and genital – from birth onwards, culminating in the Oedipus phase at age four or five.

At each developmental stage the libido centred on a different part of the body; it could become fixated at any one of the stages, resulting in psychopathology. Freud saw all individual psychopathology as being on a continuum, with neurotic patterns arising as a result of libidinal arrest at a particular stage. The aim of psychotherapy was to unravel the points of libidinal arrest so that the individual's personality could move on through the remaining developmental stages.

Freud saw the Oedipus complex as the apex of developmental stages, for it was during this stage that the libidinal drive must become fixed in its appropriate heterosexual path. The little boy and the little girl must separate from their attachment to mother in order to take their place in the world. The boy must detach his sexual feelings towards mother so that he can later reattach his sexual feelings to another woman. This detachment occurs as follows: the boy sees his father as a rival for mother's love and wishes to replace him. He wishes to castrate his father and take his place. As a result of this wish or fantasy, the little boy fears retaliation by his father, he fears castration. Fear of his own castration leads him to give up his sexual attachment to his mother by repressing or denying his sexual feelings for her. He then can take his place next to his father, and later on he will have his own woman. For the girl, resolution of the Oedipus complex and separation from mother comes about as follows: at around age three the little girl 'realizes' that she does not have a penis – she immediately thinks she has been castrated and feels the lack. The little girl feels contempt for her mother who does not have a penis and blames the mother for her own castration. The little girl's contempt and anger leads her to turn away from her mother and to attach herself to father, who has a penis, and might provide her with one. She then gives up her wish for a penis and puts in place of it a wish for a child: and with that purpose in view, she takes her father as a love object.

Concepts such as penis envy, the castration complex and the Oedipus complex, although first introduced as part of the psychoanalytic dialogue, are now common parlance and have become ideological foundation-stones upon which theories of female sexuality and female psychology are built. Freud described a feminine experience that he heard about and saw in his clinical practice. The events, feelings and nuances that he observed have provided subsequent generations with much useful material. However, Freud's observations about women's psychology and femininity were made through patriarchal spectacles. He was either unconscious of or unconcerned about his patriarchal bias, thus the theory he drew from his clinical data suffers from a particular vision. Further, having constructed a theory of female sexuality, he then superimposed it on to the clinical material. Subsequent Freudian analysts who wrote about the psychology of women have consistently maintained this bias, although they have revised the theory in other ways.

106

We have several criticisms of Freud and the post-Freudian view of women's psychology. They all stem from a bias that sees female sexuality as tied to reproduction and the gratification of male sexual impulses towards women; to women's inferiority because women and men are different; and to the control and subjugation of women. As such, the theories propose a female sexuality formed within a male image and with reference to the penis. For example, few analysts have discussed the meaning in a girl's life of her experience of her mother's body as a positive force, or of men's envy of the female body, the body from which they were all born. (Had Freud written at a different time, he might have developed a theory according to which the main focus in the psychological development of both boys and girls was on the mother's breast, the hopes that a girl would have that she would then grow up to have a mother's body, and the boy's feelings of inadequacy that he did not possess these marvellous breasts. After all, babies have far more contact with breasts than with penises.) The Freudian view of how women's psychology develops is fitted into a schema that sees female genitalia and femininity as inadequate and yet inevitable. The issue of female inadequacy, which is a starting-point for Freudian theory on femininity, flows from his patriarchal bias, that we have already mentioned.

The consequence of being raised as a daughter in patriarchal society is that women see themselves as inferior. This sense of inferiority is not formed at the Oedipus stage when the girl realizes she is not a boy [1]; it is intimately linked to the very beginning of a girl's life and the acquisition of her gender identity. This sense of gender is woven into the very fabric of earliest experience: infants are related to as girls or as boys with all that attends those terms. When a woman reveals that she feels unsatisfied, inadequate and empty she is talking about her internal experience of being a woman in our society. These feelings arise because the psychic sphere reflects that she is a woman in patriarchal culture and a second-class citizen.

Helene Deutsch, an analyst who worked closely with Freud, extended some of his lines of inquiry and argued that female passivity was a universal characteristic in women [2]. Women's activity was turned inward and contributed to the feminine attribute of intuition. For Deutsch, female sexuality was a masochistic pleasure. Orgasm is essentially a male phenomenon and the proper function of the vagina is to be passive and receptive. Intercourse for the truly feminine woman should exclude orgasm and should consist rather of slow relaxation without contractions.

This patriarchal view of women is perhaps all the more painful because it comes from a woman. Happily we know through women's own reports of their sexual experience, the work of Masters and Johnson, and women's activity and achievements in the world that this view is incorrect.

Appendix

Post-Freudians

Wilhelm Reich was the first psychoanalyst to relate individual psychology in an explicitly political way, to the world in which we live. Drawing on Engels's [3] analysis of the family he discussed how the family creates a particular psychology. He demonstrated its economic function (as a producing and consuming economic unit), its social function (as the protector of women and children deprived of economic and sexual rights), and its political function (as a training ground for bourgeois social relations in which the father is 'the exponent and representative of the authority of the State in the family') (*The Sexual Revolution*). Reich points to the psychic consequences of such an arrangement and the psychological impact of the economic subservience of women and children and female sexuality. He delineated a line of investigation that was to draw the connections between character structure and economic and social relations. His early work both in the practice and theory of psychology broke new ground and has been of tremendous inspiration to those psychotherapists interested in relating the social and psychological worlds.

In *Psychoanalysis and Feminism, Juliet Mitchell*'s reading of Freud provides a richer understanding of the girl's feelings of inadequacy at the Oedipus stage. She discusses how the girl's discovery of the anatomical differences between the sexes forces her to come to grips with the fact that she cannot win her mother's love as does her father. According to Mitchell, the girl's lack of a penis comes to mean for her that she must not only accept the loss of her first love, but also that her *active* loving is implicated in the defeat. The girl comes to see herself, her mother, and thus all women as damaged and inferior. Aware of her inferior position, she turns to father and attempts to woo him. Mitchell's account parallels Freud's in stating that boys and girls learn their place in the world in relation to their father in the Oedipus phase. Thus she explains patriarchy. Boys learn that one day they will become the father, whereas girls learn that they are both rejected by mother and will never take father's place. Juliet Mitchell has attempted to grapple with Freudian theory and has expanded it in a creative way. Her major contribution has been to discuss the whole concept of passivity and activity. She puts forward the idea that a girl has to learn passivity and give up an active pursuit of a relationship. In addition, she focuses attention on the daughter's relationship with the mother, and the loss of the mother in the girl's life.

However, neither Freud's nor Mitchell's explanation conforms to our experience in our clinical practice. We have found no evidence that how women experience themselves as incomplete or inadequate connects in any way with the fantasy of a penis or of a baby. Furthermore, we believe that femininity is part and parcel of a girl's experience from birth and not something that comes about at the Oedipus stage. We do not believe that instinctual drives of libido and aggression are what shapes human psychology.

Karen Horney, Clara Thompson, Harry Stack Sullivan and *Erich Fromm* have come to be known as the American or Cultural school of psychoanalysis. Drawing on the work of anthropologists and referring to the social conditions of the times in which they worked, Horney and Thompson in particular attempted a sociological analysis of Freud's findings on femininity. They stressed the impact of the social world on the individual's psychic structure. But they were less concerned with intrapsychic internalization of the outside world than with the impact of prevailing social attitudes on the formation of personality. For example, they looked at other cultures and saw that women's social position is subordinate in all of them. Nevertheless, the range of activities and experiences open to women differed from culture to culture. From this evidence they were therefore able to argue that femininity and masculinity are constructions intimately related to particular cultures. Although they understood the impact of cultural and social forces on child-rearing, they did not dissect the psychodynamics by which the outside world becomes transformed in its particular form in the individual psyche.

Karen Horney tried to develop a theory of women's psychology. She discussed how women were extremely interested in power and suggested that this rather than the libido was their motivating force, and that the issues which arise in the female unconscious centre around women's lack of power. She also focused attention on how men may suffer from womb envy. Clara Thompson focused on how penis envy was symbolic of women's desire for men's power and stated that women were entitled to power in the world and that there was nothing particularly healthy about a woman accepting her lot in life – concepts which were unheard of at the time.

The writings of Horney and Thompson are both accessible and exciting to read. They were revolutionaries within the psychoanalytic community, and they were the first people to bring a feminist perspective into psychoanalysis. Their weakness, from our point of view as working therapists, is that they were not able to explain the particularities of female psychology. Nevertheless they did break new ground, by offering a woman-oriented perspective on women's psychology.

Instinctually-based Object Relations Theorists and Ego Psychologists

The work of Melanie Klein in the analysis of young children led her to a decisive intellectual breakthrough in psychoanalytic thinking. While maintaining the stress on instinctual forces, and in particular the death instinct in the organization of psychic life, her detailed examination of the fantasy and play of children provided a richer interpretation of Freudian theory. Focusing her attention on the first years of life, she described the inner world of the child and how its mental life was organized.

Klein stressed the development of the ego as the core of personal life. In this she side-tracked, but she did not abandon the topography of Freud's id and super-ego. The ego was the centre of the developing child's world. It was the ego, as it came to stand for the person, that had an intensely private life with the people, or, to use her words, the 'objects', to whom it related. For Klein, the instincts sought objects as their aim, rather than pleasure as Freud posited. The objects, i.e. the people, were, however, objects of an internal nature rather than images of the actual people in the child's life. The internal objects were part of the heritage that an infant brought into the world along with instincts. Where an instinct arose so did an image of an object to satisfy it. Real people were screens upon which the infant could project its internal fantasies. Experience of people in the world confirmed the experience of the child's internal object relations. Klein explained the inner fantasy world in terms of the struggle between the two great instincts: libido – the life force – and aggression – the death instinct. These two instinctual forces met in the individual's psyche and formed the battleground on which the ego developed. Klein discussed how, at the beginning of life, the baby begins to take into itself the good experiences at the breast and to project from itself on to the breast the bad experiences. Thus the mother's breast, and later, when the infant can experience a whole person, the mother, becomes both the good and the bad object. In later life, all people intimately connected with the person become a projection screen for the internal objects of the individual's psyche.

What Klein saw in her practice was in fact much richer than her explanation claims, for her observations are continually short-circuited by the insistence on inner psychic life as instinctual rather than social. For feminism, the most profound of her discoveries lies in the early object relationships of mother-raised children. Her shift of emphasis to early life and the construction of personality in the first few years brings into the arena (although Klein herself does not emphasize this) the importance of the early acquisition of femininity and masculinity, long before the Freudian Oedipus phase. Another important discovery of Klein's early object relations is forcefully argued by Dorothy Dinnerstein, in *The Mermaid and the Minotaur*. Her argument runs: since all infants organize their internal life around the person of the mother, and all infants have good and bad experiences at the mother's breast and in her social arena, and since all infants come to identify with the person of the caretaker who is at once both the loved one and the feared and hated one, then all children raised by women take into themselves a picture of woman as both all-good and powerful on the one hand and all-bad and withholding on the other. Dinnerstein, using Kleinian theory, thus explains the misogynist nature of all our psychologies.

The work of the ego psychologists similarly focused on the early internalizations and structuralizations of the ego. *Margaret Mahler* and her colleagues observed many infant–caretaker interactions and drew a picture of the transition from infant to toddler, stressing the development of psychic structuralization. Mahler saw that the baby becomes human within human relationships, that the psychological birth of the human infant is a process that occurs outside the womb and is shaped in relationship.

Ronald Fairbairn was the first analyst to depart radically from Freud's instinct theory and to revise libido theory. Fairbairn developed an object relations theory of ego development based on social relationships. He was greatly influenced by the work of Melanie Klein, but whereas Klein maintained instincts theory and placed much emphasis on the world of internalized objects, Fairbairn dismissed the notion of instincts as primary determinants in the formation of the psyche, and posited a materialist view of ego development.

Fairbairn believed that the significance of the object to the person was not as a means of instinctual gratification, but in terms of its essential place in the development of the ego. Fairbairn believed that the ego, the person, the self, *develops only* in relationships. Whereas Freud saw libido as primarily seeking satisfaction, Fairbairn believed that the individual has a drive for relationship, a drive for contact with another human being. Thus the infant has a primary need for human contact. Ego development begins at birth and in relation to the primary caretaker, the mother. The mother is the most constant person in the infant's world. This early period, which Fairbairn calls 'infantile dependence', is the pivotal period in ego development. (See Chapter 1 for our integration of Fairbairn's developmental theory.)

Fairbairn saw that in the course of ego development a part of the person withdraws and goes into hiding. Fairbairn calls this 'withdrawal', this split in the ego, the 'schizoid' split, and it is a major part of his work on schizoid personalities.

In discussing the schizoid personality Fairbairn says that anxiety arises out of the experience of not having needs attended to. In order to deal with the anxiety, the person denies the need. In denying the need, the person is cutting off a part of him or herself, hiding it from the outer world and relationships. The split ego, one part of which has now withdrawn into an inner world, experiences a sense of futility and hopelessness. The longed-for, potentially satisfying object seems further and further away. In adult life, the schizoid person (and we should add here that to some extent everyone has a schizoid split) feels her or himself to have a private part of their personality which is kept hidden from others. The person may feel there is one part of her or himself which is in the world and seen by others, but often feels this part is somehow inauthentic. The schizoid person often feels cut off and apart from other people. Only within intimate, safe relationships does the hidden part have the possibility of emerging.

W. D. Winnicott. Winnicott's professional interest in psychoanalysis evolved from his experience of working with children as a paediatrician, and so the insights and the far-reaching effects of his work were built upon his observations of the early relationship between infant and mother. Winnicott's emphasis was on the very early stages of life outside the womb. Although very much in the psychoanalytic tradition, his work was a decisive shift away from the formulations of Freud and Klein, for he was in essence a materialist. His famous remark, 'There is no such thing as an infant, meaning, of course, that wherever one finds an infant one finds maternal care, and without maternal care there would be no infant', places the emphasis on the relationship between infant and caretaker that allows the baby to become a person. Winnicott coined the phrase 'ego relatedness' by which he meant the capacity of the ego to develop a sense of security within itself and its environment through good enough mothering.

Focusing on the period just before and after birth, he writes of the identification mothers feel with their infants, their capacity to empathize, to provide a psychic umbilical cord that nourishes the developing ego.

He wrote about the true self and the false self. The true self is the very core of human existence, the capacity to relate to oneself and others. The false self arises as a protection against an undernourished ego that feels no security. Shortcomings or failures in early maternal nurturance lead to false selves, and inhibit the development of a whole ego.

Winnicott made a major contribution to the theory and practice of psychotherapy. He implemented in his therapeutic work the understandings of early processes: 'My thesis is that what we do in therapy is to attempt to imitate the natural process that characterises the behaviour of any mother with her own infant. It is the mother–infant couple that can teach us the basic principles on which we may base our therapeutic work.' Again, while Winnicott's work is extremely useful, he accepts that the pattern of child-rearing in contemporary society is sound, and that the problems caused by poor mothering relate only to a fault in the mother-child relationship, rather than to flaws in present child-rearing arrangements.

Harry Guntrip, an analysand of Fairbairn, took up the contributions of Fairbairn and Winnicott and extended the analysis of the developmental stage of schizoid phenomena. In other words, he understood that this early dynamic of splitting was critical in the formation of aspects of the personality. His modesty and clear exposition of Fairbairn's and Winnicott's work makes it difficult to know where his particular contribution started and theirs ended. Most striking is the humanity he brought to his understanding of the person and the relationship of self and others. Guntrip's clinical work is clearly of a radical nature. He was most insistent on the quality of the therapeutic relationship and the need for the therapist to locate the unintegrated or hidden self that the schizoid personality reveals in the safety of a trusting relationship. He, along with Winnicott, saw therapy with distressed people as repair work that would restart the maturational processes that had been halted. What comes across clearly in Guntrip's descriptions of his work and clients is the importance of nurturance within the therapy relationship. This concept is a cornerstone of our feminist psychotherapy.

While our theory shares much with the work of Fairbairn, Guntrip and Winnicott we must stress where we diverge from the object relations theorists. For we acknowledge that mother is not an object, mother is a person, a social and psychological being. What becomes internalized from this perspective then is not the object, but the different aspects of mother. What the object relations theorists have failed to take into account is the psychology of the mother and the effect of the social position of women on the mother's psychology.

Notes

Introduction to Feminist Psychotherapy

1. Phyllis Chesler, New York, 1972, London, 1974.
2. See Phil Brown (ed.), *Radical Psychology*, New York, 1973; Jerome Agel, *The Radical Therapist*, New York, 1971.
3. Pauline Bart, 'Depression in Middle-Aged Women', in: V. Gornick and B. K. Moran (eds.), *Women in Sexist Society*, New York, 1971.
4. I. K. Broverman, D. M. Broverman, F. E. Clarkson, P. S. Rosenkrantz and S. R. Vogel, 'Sex-Role Stereotypes in Clinical Judgements of Mental Health', *Journal of Consulting and Clinical Psychology*, Vol. 34, 1970, pp. 1–7.
5. See *International Journal of Psychoanalysis*, Vol. 57, 1976.
6. See, for example, S. Freud, *Civilization and Its Discontents*, London and New York, 1930.
7. See *Critique of Anthropology*, Vol. 3, 1977; Eleanor Burke Leacock (Introduction to), *The Origin of the Family, Private Property and the State* (by Friedrich Engels), New York, 1972.
8. J. Chasseguet-Smirgel, *Female Sexuality*, Ann Arbor, Mich., 1970.
9. See, for example, Shere Hite, *The Hite Report*, New York and London, 1977.
10. A bias that had progressive elements at the time, particularly in view of the intellectual climate of the late 1950s in the United States. See particularly Betty Friedan, *The Feminine Mystique* (1963), for what Freudianism had come to mean about women's psychology in that period.
11. See, for example, Hogie Wycoff, *Solving Women's Problems*, New York, 1977.
12. See, for example, S. Orbach, *Fat is a Feminist Issue*, London, 1978; S. Ernst and L. Goodison, *In Our Own Hands*, London, 1981.
Teresa Bernardez-Bonesatti, a feminist psychiatrist, makes a provocative point when, in a study of sixty women, she discusses the developmental levels of feminist and non-feminist women seeking psychotherapy. She argues that the experience of consciousness-raising has enabled feminist women to express their anger and move towards separation–individuation (*Heresies*, No. 2, May 1977).
13. We reject the interpretation of unconscious material being specifically and necessarily Oedipal. This is in sharp contrast to the work of those feminists who have reinterpreted Freud in terms of Lacan and come to an understanding of women's subservience based on their entry into patriarchal culture at the Oedipal stage. See J. Mitchell, *Psychoanalysis and Feminism*, London, 1975. Jean Strouse's excellent collection, *Women and Analysis* (1974), was not given

as much attention, although it provided a more comprehensive rethinking of Freud.

14. N. Chodorow, *The Reproduction of Mothering*, Berkeley, 1978.

15. N. Friday, *My Mother, My Self*, New York, 1977, London, 1979.

16. A. Rich, *Of Woman Born*, New York, 1976, London, 1977.

17. S. Hammer, *Daughters and Mothers, Mothers and Daughters*, New York, 1975.

Chapter I

1. The process of psychological development occurs within the relationship of infant and caretaker. We will be talking about mothers when we speak of the caretaker because of the social structure of the nuclear family and child-rearing in our culture, which has women in the position of mother and for the most part sole child-rearer.

2. The term ego is used by different schools of psychoanalysis in different ways. We use ego to mean the emotional and psychological life of the person, including unconscious and conscious aspects of the personality. The ego is the whole psychic structure, as opposed to Freud's construction of id, ego, super-ego.

3. See R. A. Spitz, *The First Year of Life: A Psychoanalytic Study of Normal and Deviant Development of Object Relations*, New York, 1965.

4. M. S. Mahler, *et al.*, *The Psychological Birth of the Human Infant: Symbiosis and Individuation*, New York and London, 1975.

5. D. W. Winnicott, 'The Capacity to be Alone', *International Journal of Psychoanalysis*, Vol. 39, 1958, pp. 416–20.

6. See the work of Fairbairn and Guntrip on schizoid phenomena.

7. This is, of course, changing, now that some fathers are consciously involved in child-rearing either as a part of a nuclear family or in innovative familial arrangements.

8. On this point we are in some disagreement with Robert Stoller and Nancy Chodorow, who focus on the difficulties boys have in separation because of their original merger with mother. They believe boys' separation difficulties are compounded by this gender difference, whereas we believe their gender difference *aids* them in separation.

9. R. J. Stoller, *Sex and Gender*, New York, 1968, London, 1969.

10. The anthropological studies of Margaret Mead show the plasticity of these variations in cross-cultural settings. She observed that 'in all cultures, without any exception, male activity is seen as achievement; whatever women do – gathering seeds, planting, weeding, basket-making, pot-making – is valued less than when the same activity in some other culture is performed by men' (*Women and Analysis*, ed. Jean Strouse). Further, she discovered that in one culture a quality has been assigned to females and in another it is praised as a male attribute: 'Now it is boys who are thought of as infinitely vulnerable and in need of special cherishing care, now it is girls. In some societies it is girls for whom parents must collect a dowry or make husband-catching magic, in others the parents' worry is over the difficulty of marrying off the boys' (*Male and Female*, Harmondsworth, Penguin Books, 1976, p. 30).

11. This assertion is a direct challenge to previous views in psychoanalysis on the development of masculinity and femininity. For Freud a child was bisexual for the first years of life and at the Oedipal phase (age four or five) the girl or boy came to know itself as feminine or masculine. One strain in the post-Freudian view of psychosexual development posited that human beings are born with masculine or feminine sexuality. Both positions are based on the belief that biological sex determines masculinity or femininity. Work in the area of gender identity, then, has been of particular interest to feminists, for its findings are a direct challenge to the idea that biology determines psychology.

12. J. Money and A. Erhardt, *Man and Woman, Boy and Girl: The Differentiation and Dimorphism of Gender Identity from Conception to Maturity*, Baltimore, Md, 1972, London, 1973.

Chapter II

1. Winnicott, in describing the mother's ability to respond to her infant's needs in the first year of life, writes: 'Towards the end of the pregnancy and for a few weeks after the birth of a child the mother is preoccupied with (or better "given over to") the care of her baby, which at first seems like a part of herself; moreover she is very much identified with the baby and knows quite well what the baby is feeling like. For this she uses her own experience as a baby' (*Dependence Towards Independence*, 1963). Winnicott writes of the mother's primary maternal preoccupation as an 'extraordinary condition which is almost like an illness . . .' (*The Family and Individual Development*, London, Tavistock, 1965, pp. 15–16). In the period of the mother providing for the needs of the infant, she is herself vulnerable: 'In finding the part of her that identifies with the infant, the mother is herself in a dependent state and vulnerable' (*The Maturational Processes and the Facilitating Environment*, London, 1963).

2. Nancy Friday, *My Mother, My Self*, New York, 1977, London, 1979.

3. Adrienne Rich, *Of Woman Born*, New York, 1976, London, 1977.

4. Men's psychology is obviously not the subject of this book but for an explication of men's fear of women see: Robert J. Stoller, *Sex and Gender*, New York, 1968, London, 1969; Dorothy Dinnerstein, *The Rocking of the Cradle, and the Ruling of the World*, London, 1978 (first published, in New York, 1976, as *The Mermaid and the Minotaur*).

Chapter III

1. For a summary of contemporary positions on transference, countertransference and the therapy relationship, see *The Patient and The Analyst* by J. Sandler, C. Dare and A. Holden, London, 1973.

2. We describe our practice at the Women's Therapy Centre, where the relationship has been that of two women. This raises the interesting point that has been put to us a number of times about whether a man can be a feminist therapist, and provide this reparative relationship for a woman in therapy.

3. The school of psychotherapy within which she works, e.g. psychoanalytic, gestalt etc.

4. See Chapter VII, 'Dynamics between Couples and Implications for Couple Counselling'.

Chapter IV

1. Supervision refers to the practice of discussing with a colleague or colleagues one's clinical work in distinct ways: as a monitoring device for technical advice, and an arena for the exploration of the therapist's countertransference issues.

2. The therapist herself is often unaware that the views she holds are informed by a particular class and ethnic perspective. Because of the power differential in the therapy relationship the therapist may unwittingly act as a conveyor of such views and influence the therapy in a particular direction. Therapists are constantly evaluating what is happening with their clients in terms of the shift in the client's intra-psychic life and her interface with the world. Awareness of class and ethnic issues is extremely important if the therapist is to be sensitive, without prejudice, to the life-style choices that a particular woman might make. We have found the following points useful in discussing issues of class and ethnicity in post-graduate training workshops at the Women's Therapy Centre.

Points to discuss

(a) The therapist's treatment goals may be based on her notion of what is appropriate for that class or that ethnic group.

(b) The selection of clients is frequently made by criteria that, seemingly value-free on the surface, are in fact ideological, e.g. therapists often remark that potential clients are 'bright' or 'motivated', when what they are responding to is verbal ability and articulateness, which they seem surprised to encounter in working-class women or women from cultures different from their own.

Working-class Black and Asian people are taken on for therapy more easily if they exhibit middle-class characteristics.

(c) Therapists are often blind to the issues of class and race that clients present, perhaps 'psychologizing' or interpreting them. Because of this, the therapist may not adequately explore with her clients their ethnic and class backgrounds, thus missing crucial issues for the client.

(d) Therapists can be unaware of how their own class and ethnic background contributes to the shape of the therapy and of how inequalities stemming from it can emerge in the therapy relationship. Therapists can be defensive if they have not explored their own attitudes to class and ethnicity.

(e) An aspect of psychotherapy training places an emphasis on the difference between *us* (therapists) and *them* (clients). Perhaps therapists utilize class and ethnic differences in this distancing from the client. In addition, in many training programmes there is no provision for discussion of issues of class and race, as though they were irrelevant to the personality of the person and unimportant in the therapy. Such issues that do come up can often be seen to be exclusively issues of countertransference and transference and, therefore, delegitimated as issues in themselves.

In our workshop we focus on these general themes and then move on to explore our own attitudes. We consider:

(a) Our own class and ethnic background and our awareness of it.

(b) The background of our own therapist and its role in our own therapy.

(c) The background of our supervisor and how it influenced us.

(d) The ideas we hold about Black people, Asian people, immigrants from Europe to England, working-class people, Irish people and therapy.

(e) The need to rethink our work with clients in the light of the potential tensions that arise around class and ethnicity.

3. We developed the following peer-group supervision model for a conference of psychotherapists held in London in April 1978 (The Feminist Therapist Training Group):

Step One: One of the therapists describes a client she is working with, giving details of her family, class and ethnic background, her current situation, her sexual orientation, her presenting problems on entering therapy and the course of the therapy so far. *Step Two:* The therapists share their identification with the client, discussing the areas in the client's life that resemble their own and noting any points in the presentation when the therapists were particularly moved. *Step Three:* We suggest that the therapists ask themselves the following questions: How do they understand the woman's distress? What does this distress have to do with the experience of being a woman? How is her gender central to what she is experiencing? How does the presenting problem or distress relate to her struggle to be an adult woman? *Step Four:* We ask technical questions: How would we work with this particular client? What would the therapy goals be? What is happening in the transference? How would we distinguish between countertransference and identification? How do we understand the mother–daughter relationship and its developmental implications for girls? We ask for specific suggestions about directions to go in and technical innovations, etc. *Step Five:* About a month after initial discussions the therapist reports to the group on what has happened in the sessions after initial presentation.

Another model discussed at this conference was the result of work done by a feminist study group in New York City. It proposed a practicum: in other words, the women in the group would practise on each other. Each week one woman would present a problem from her own life, as in a therapy session. She would be the client. She could either choose one of the other women to be the therapist, or work therapeutically in the group as a whole. This is a vulnerable and self-exposing exercise. As therapists usually work in isolation, no one really knows what goes on in someone else's sessions. This method breaks down some of this isolation.

The group recommended that the session be conducted as if it were a normal therapy session with a client. Then the group as a whole would focus on certain issues. For example, how could the woman's feelings be connected with the objective political circumstances? How could the therapist have interpreted what was presented differently? How would a traditional therapist view it? How had the therapists exposed their own supporting ideology in the sessions? How else could the therapists have viewed the issue? How else could they have handled the material? Where do the implicit values of the therapist emanate from? Are they in the interests of the client? Are they in the interests of the therapist? The members suggested that the sessions be taped, so that the transactions in the session could be examined in detail.

These two models for peer supervision can provide a forum for a frank discussion of the issues facing therapists. We think it extremely important for the therapist to have a place where she can discharge her reactions to her sessions, for several reasons. One is, as we have discussed, the issue of identification versus countertransference; the second is that therapists need a place to discuss the feelings they experience in the course of their work. We think it is particularly difficult for the therapist to encourage a client to express feelings of distress (often within the transference) unless the therapist also has a place where she can express those feelings herself. This applies equally to the feelings of intimacy that develop between two people working together. Boundary issues are a major problem for women and a prerequisite of competent therapy is that the therapist be alert to where her emotional life begins and ends in relation to the help she can offer her client. Finally, it is useful for the therapist to have an arena in which to discuss how she feels about carrying the dependencies of the numerous women with whom she works, inasmuch as, again, these feelings cannot be dealt with solely in transference.

Chapter V

1. Obviously class is in itself an extremely complex category in relation to women, for a woman's class has always been defined in relation to her husband's or father's class.

2. In addition, colleagues have held workshops on such topics as guilt, ageing, fathers and daughters, body image, mothers and children. About twelve workshops take place in any one week and on average one hundred women attend such groups weekly.

3. Some of the groups at the Women's Therapy Centre are designed to become leaderless self-help groups and are structured along those lines. See Sheila Ernst and Lucy Goodison, *In Our Own Hands*, London, 1981.

4. In a factory there may be only women on an assembly line but this structure is created by managers, who tend to be men. In the household, a woman may be with her women friends but that does not make it a woman-only environment, because it is a relegation.

5. The form of the women's group evolves, of course, from the Women's Liberation Movement, where women first sought out other women and met in consciousness-raising or 'rap' groups as a way to understand their individual and isolated experience.

6. See Jean Baker Miller, *Towards a New Psychology of Women,* Boston, Mass., 1976, for a discussion of such positive aspects of women's experience that are deeply a part of each woman's psychology.

7. Perhaps the very possibility of being in a situation in which she could explore her desires and ambition provided an opening.

8. In a women-only therapy group, because women are not having to compete with or against the men, the feelings of being a second-class citizen, of being invalid within a group, have less opportunity to be reinforced. A single-sex group makes for very different power dynamics. The introduction of a man into a group of women breaks and changes this dynamic.

A mixed therapy group run by a feminist therapist will be aware of the meaning of gender in the group dynamics. With a feminist perspective one is aware of: the sexual politics of the group; how the presence of women and men affects each of the sexes; how women relate to men; how women relate to women when men are present; how men relate to women; and, of course, how men relate with each other when women are present. One is also aware that the women may select different material in a mixed therapy group than when in a women's therapy group. There are many points to be made about a feminist perspective on mixed groups, but this is not the subject at this point. Let us just focus on three issues to look at in leading a mixed group. One: what happens when a man actually opens up in the therapy group? Who is attentive to him, who nurtures him? Is it the women, is it the men? Do the men feel inadequate at nurturing, and are, therefore, the women taking on the nurturing role, or is that challenged within the group? Similarly, how do men cope with women's upset and neediness in the group? Do they run away from it and leave other women to cope with it, or do they struggle with their own fears and inadequacies?

How is competition manifested in the mixed group? – between the women and the men, and between the men and the men.

This is a very interesting aspect of sexual politics to look at. In addition, of course, you get a tremendous amount of anger stirring. Men's anger at women for being so powerful and so withholding and all the images of womanhood and women's sexuality, and, of course, women's anger and women's placatory stance towards men. So a feminist therapist can be very helpful in pinpointing these dynamics in a mixed-therapy group.

In our post-graduate training workshops at the Women's Therapy Centre, we look at the following questions:

(a) Who takes space in the group (issues related to this)?

(b) Who takes care of whom in mixed therapy groups?

(c) How do women and men relate differentially to either a woman or man therapist?

(d) How are issues around women's autonomy or connectedness experienced by group members and how are they interpreted by the therapist?

(e) Is there anxiety in the group related to women's separateness?

(f) How is female/male sexuality worked on in groups?

(g) Are issues around vulnerability more difficult for men? Do they feel they must maintain an image?

(h) What do women in group feel about men's vulnerability or feelings of inadequacy?

Notes

(i) How does a feminist analysis of the family and power relations based on sexual lines affect interpretations of group dynamics?

(j) How does a feminist analysis of the family affect transference interpretations in relation to both the therapist and other group members?

Chapter VI

1. Joy Melville, *Phobias and Obsessions,* London, 1977.

2. Jean Baker Miller, *Psychoanalysis and Women,* London, 1973.

3. See Susie Orbach, *Fat is a Feminist Issue,* London, 1978, and 'Compulsive Eating in Women', *British Journal of Sexual Medicine*, March 1981, for a picture of the psychosocial analysis of compulsive eating for women. For a more detailed discussion of anorexia see: Hilde Bruch, *Eating Disorders,* New York, 1973; Sheila Macleod, *The Art of Starvation,* London, 1981; Susie Orbach, 'Anorexia in Women', *British Journal of Sexual Medicine*, July 1981; Mara Selvini Palazzoli, *Self-Starvation,* London, 1974.

Chapter VII

1. The perspective we offer here comes from our own experience in a couples group from July 1978 to July 1980. The other participants were Andrew Friend, Joseph Schwartz, Sally Berry and Tom Ryan.

In our post-graduate training workshops at the Women's Therapy Centre, we have used the following points to sensitize psychotherapists to the dynamics between couples.

(a) *Issues related to intimacy.* Why is intimacy so difficult to achieve? What are the fears associated with emotional intimacy?

(i) Psychological fits: What makes people attracted to one another? Are there emotional fits that work/that do not work between people?

(ii) Boundary issues: Does one person keep tight boundaries as a protection against intimacy while the other partner reaches out in search of contact? Does intimacy feel like merger and loss of self? Does one person 'take over' the other and possess them? Is it possible to have two whole separated people together in a couple?

(iii) The cha-cha phenomenon.

(b) *Dependency.* Why does it so often appear to be one person who is more dependent in the relationship than the other partner? Why is this person more often than not the woman (if there is a man and a woman in relationship)? Is it possible to achieve interdependency in intimate relationships? What are the issues the therapist takes up and how?

(i) The effect of women's lack of separateness in couples: Does the woman's lack of separateness provide the safety net for the man to be more separate?

(ii) Do men's difficulties with nurturing hamper women's activities away from home and in the world?

(iii) What, if anything, does women's autonomy and psychological separateness do in relationships? What is the impact of women's autonomy?

(c) *Sexuality*. What are the difficulties with achieving sexual intimacy for couples? Are the issues different or the same for lesbian and heterosexual intimacy? If not, what are the differences? Where does sex fit into intimacy? How do women's and men's deeply held views about female sexuality affect sexual relationships between men and women?

Chapter VIII

1. Simone de Beauvoir, *The Second Sex*, New York, 1952, Harmondsworth, Penguin Books, 1972.

2. See Robert J. Stoller, *Sex and Gender*, New York, 1968, London, 1969; Dorothy Dinnerstein, *The Mermaid and the Minotaur*, New York, 1976 (UK title: *The Rocking of the Cradle and the Ruling of the World*, London, 1978).

3. See Diane Ohrensaft, 'When Women and Men Mother', *Socialist Review*, January 1980, pp. 837–73.

Appendix

1. Perhaps this is a good example of Freud's unconscious defensive stance upon realizing that he was not like his mother, not a woman. Perhaps he felt terribly inadequate when he realized that he would not grow breasts or be able to bear children!

2. See Helene Deutsch, *The Psychology of Women*, Vols. 1 and 2, New York, 1944, 1945; Marie Bonaparte, *Female Sexuality*, New York, 1953.

3. Friedrich Engels, writing in 1884 in *The Origin of the Family, Private Property and the State*, completely reversed the prevailing view of the family. Drawing on the available anthropological data of Bachofen and the writing of Henry Morgan, Engels persuasively argues a materialist basis for changing a family structure that still persists today, virtually unchanged, i.e. the modern nuclear family and monogamous marriage. The development of the nuclear family 'is not the reconciliation of man and woman . . . quite the contrary, monogamous marriage comes on the scene as the subjugation of the one sex by the other . . . and the first class oppression coincides with that of the female sex by the male'.

Bibliography

Arcana, Judith, *Our Mother Daughters*, Berkeley, Calif., 1979.

Aries, Philippe, *Centuries of Childhood: A Social History of Family Life*, New York, 1960.

Baker Miller, Jean, *Psychoanalysis and Women*, London, 1973.

Baker Miller, Jean, *Towards a New Psychology of Women*, Boston, Mass., 1976.

Balint, Alice, *The Early Years of Life: A Psychoanalytic Study*, New York, 1954.

Barber, Virginia, and Skaggs, Merrill Maguire, *The Mother Person*, New York and London, 1977.

Bardwick, Judith, *Psychology of Women: A Study of Bio-cultural Conflicts*, New York, 1971.

Belotti, Elena Gianini, *Little Girls*, London, 1975.

Bernard, Jessie, *The Future of Marriage*, New York, 1972.

Bernard, Jessie, *The Future of Motherhood*, New York, 1974.

Blanck and Blanck, *Ego Psychology: Theory and Practice*, New York, 1974.

Bowlby, John, *Attachment and Loss*, Vols. 1 & 2, London, 1969, 1973.

Broverman, I. K., Vogel, S. R., Broverman, D. M., Clarkson, F. E. and Rosenkrantz, P. S., 'Sex Role Stereotypes: A Current Appraisal', *Journal of Social Issues*, Vol. 28, No. 2, 1972, pp. 59–78.

Brown, Bruce, *Marx, Freud and the Critique of Everyday Life*, New York and London, 1973.

Brownmiller, Susan, *Against Our Will. Men, Women and Rape*, New York and London, 1975.

Chasseguet-Smirgel, Janine, *Female Sexuality*, Ann Arbor, Mich., 1970.

Chesler, Phyllis, *Women and Madness*, New York, 1972, London, 1974.

Chodorow, Nancy, *The Reproduction of Mothering: Psychoanalysis and the Sociology of Gender*, Berkeley, Calif., 1978.

Daly, A., *Mothers*, London, 1976.

de Beauvoir, Simone, *The Second Sex*, New York, 1952, Harmondsworth, 1972.

Deutsch, Helene, *The Psychology of Women*, Vols. 1 and 2, New York, 1944, 1945.

Dinnerstein, Dorothy, *The Mermaid and the Minotaur; Sexual Arrangements and Human Malaise*, New York, 1976. Published in London, 1978, as *The Rocking of the Cradle and the Ruling of the World*.

Engels, Friedrich, *The Origin of the Family, Private Property and the State*, New York, 1973, London, 1978.

Erikson, Erik, 'Womanhood and the Inner Space' in Robert Jay Lifton (ed.), *The*

Bibliography

Woman in America, Boston, Mass., 1964, London, 1977.

Ernst, Sheila, and Goodison, Lucy, In Our Own Hands, London, 1981.

Fairbairn, W. R. D., Psychoanalytic Studies of the Personality, London, 1952.

Fenichel, O., Psychoanalytic Theory of Neurosis, New York, 1945, London, 1946.

Foucault, Michel, The History of Sexuality, Vol. I. An Introduction, New York, 1978.

Freud, Anna, The Ego and the Mechanisms of Defense, New York, 1966, London, 1968.

Freud, Sigmund, The Complete Psychological Works, London, 1953 (Standard Edition). (See also the Pelican Freud Library.)

Friday, Nancy, My Mother, My Self, New York, 1977, London, 1979.

Friedan, Betty, The Feminine Mystique, New York, 1963, Harmondsworth, 1965.

Frieze, Parsons, Johnson, Ruble, Zellman, Women and Sex Roles. A Social Psychological Perspective, New York, 1978.

Gagnon, John H., and Simon, William, Sexual Conduct: The Social Sources of Human Sexuality, Chicago, 1973.

Garfield Barback, Lonnie, For Yourself: The Fulfillment of Female Sexuality, New York, 1975.

Gornick, Vivian, and Moran, Barbara K. (eds.), Woman in Sexist Society: Studies in Power and Powerlessness, New York, 1971.

Guntrip, Harry, Personality Structure and Human Interaction: The Developing Synthesis of Psychodynamic Theory, New York and London, 1961.

Guntrip, Harry, Schizoid Phenomena and Object Relations Theory, London, 1968.

Guntrip, Harry, Psychoanalytic Theory, Therapy and the Self, New York and London, 1971.

Hammer, Signe, Daughters and Mothers, Mothers and Daughters, New York, 1975.

Hammer, Signe, Women, Body and Culture, New York, 1975.

Hartmann, Heinz, Ego Psychology and the Problem of Adaptation, New York, 1958.

Hershberger, Ruth, Adam's Rib, New York, 1948.

Hite, Shere, The Hite Report, New York and London, 1977.

Horney, Karen, Feminine Psychology, New York, 1967.

Jacobson, Edith, The Self and the Object World, New York, 1964.

Jacoby, Russell, Social Amnesia, Boston, Mass., 1975, London, 1977.

Kaplan, J. L., Oneness and Separateness, From Infant to Individual, New York, 1978.

Kernberg, Otto, Borderline Conditions and Pathological Narcissism, New York, 1975.

Kernberg, Otto, Object Relations Theory and Clinical Psychoanalysis, New York, 1976.

Klein, George S., Freud's Two Theories of Sexuality: Psychological Issues, No. 9.

Klein, Melanie, Envy and Gratitude, New York and London, 1975.

Klein, Melanie, et al., Developments in Psychoanalysis, London, 1952.

Lazarre, Jane, The Mother Knot, New York, 1976.

Maccoby, Eleanor, and Jacklin, Carol, The Psychology of Sex Differences, Stanford, Calif., 1974.

Mahler, Margaret S., Pine, Fred, and Bergman, Anni, The Psychological Birth of the

Human Infant: Symbiosis and Individuation, New York and London, 1975.

Mahler, Margaret, *On Human Symbiosis and the Vicissitudes of Individuation*, New York, 1964.

Masters, William H., and Johnson, Virginia E., *Human Sexual Response*, Boston, Mass., 1966.

Mead, Margaret, *Male and Female*, Harmondsworth, 1962, New York, 1968.

Millett, Kate, *Sexual Politics*, New York and London, 1971.

Mitchell, Juliet, *Women's Estate*, New York and Harmondsworth, 1971.

Mitchell, Juliet, *Psychoanalysis and Feminism*, New York, 1974, and London, 1975.

Money, John, and Erhardt, Anke, *Man and Woman, Boy and Girl: The Differentiation and Dimorphism of Gender Identity from Conception to Maturity*, Baltimore, Md., 1972, London, 1973.

Money, John, and Tucker, Patricia, *Sexual Signatures: On Being a Man or a Woman*, London, 1977.

Oakley, Ann, *Sex, Gender and Society*, London, 1972.

Orbach, Susie, *Fat is a Feminist Issue*, London and New York, 1978.

Orbach, Susie, *Fat is a Feminist Issue II*, London, 1982.

Person, Ethel, *Sexuality as the mainstay of identity: Psychoanalytic perspectives, Signs*, Summer 1980, 605–630.

Reich, Wilhelm, *Character Analysis*, London, 1933.

Reich, Wilhelm, *The Mass Psychology of Fascism*, London, 1933.

Reich, Wilhelm, *The Sexual Revolution*, London, 1929–35.

Reich, Wilhelm, and Teschitz, K., *Selected Sex-Pol Essays, 1934–37*, London, 1973.

Reitz, Rosetta, *Menopause: A Positive Approach*, London, 1979.

Rich, Adrienne, *Of Woman Born: Motherhood as Experience and Institution*, New York, 1976, London, 1977.

Schneider, Michael, *Neurosis and Civilization: A Marxist-Freudian Synthesis*, New York, 1975.

Searles, Harold, *Collected Papers on Schizophrenia and Related Subjects*, London, 1965.

Segal, Hanna, *Introduction to the Work of Melanie Klein*, London, 1964.

Sharpe, Sue, *Just Like a Girl: How Girls Learn to be Women*, London, 1976.

Sherfey, Mary Jane, *The Nature and Evolution of Female Sexuality*, New York, 1966.

Shuttle, Penelope, and Redgrove, Peter, *The Wise Wound. Menstruation and Every Woman*, London, 1978.

Spitz, Rene A., *The First Year of Life: A Psychoanalytic Study of Normal and Deviant Development of Object Relations*, New York, 1965.

Stoller, Robert J., *Sex and Gender: On the Development of Masculinity and Femininity*, New York, 1968, London, 1969.

Stoller, Robert J., *Splitting: A Case of Female Masculinity*, New York, 1973, London, 1974.

Strouse, Jean, *Women and Analysis*, New York, 1974.

Sullivan, Harry Stack, *The Interpersonal Theory of Psychiatry*, New York, 1953.

Thompson, Clara, *Psychoanalysis: Evolution and Development*, New York, 1957.

127

Bibliography

Thompson, Clara, *On Women*, New York, 1964.

Thompson, Clara, *Interpersonal Psychoanalysis: The Selected Papers of Clara Thompson*, New York, 1964.

Weideger, Paula, *Female Cycles*, New York, 1975, London, 1978.

Williams, Elizabeth Friar, *Notes of a Feminist Therapist*, New York, 1977.

Winnicott, D. W., *Primary Maternal Preoccupation: Collected Papers*, London, 1978.

Winnicott, D. W., *The Maturational Processes and the Facilitating Environment*, London, 1963.

Winnicott, D. W., *The Family and Individual Development*, London and New York, 1965.

Winnicott, D. W., *The Child, The Family and the Outside World*, London, 1964.

Zaretsky, Eli, *Capitalism, the Family and Personal Life*, New York and London, 1976.

Zimbalist Rosaldo, Michelle, and Lamphere, Louise, *Woman, Culture and Society*, Stanford, Calif., 1974.

Index

More about Penguins and Pelicans

For further information about books available from Penguins please write to Dept EP, Penguin Books Ltd, Harmondsworth, Middlesex UB7 0DA.

In the U.S.A.: For a complete list of books available from Penguins in the United States write to Dept CS, Penguin Books, 625 Madison Avenue, New York, New York 10022.

In Canada: For a complete list of books available from Penguins in Canada write to Penguin Books Canada Ltd, 2801 John Street, Markham, Ontario L3R 1B4.

In Australia: For a complete list of books available from Penguins in Australia write to the Marketing Department, Penguin Books Australia Ltd, P.O. Box 257, Ringwood, Victoria 3134.

In New Zealand: For a complete list of books available from Penguins in New Zealand write to the Marketing Department, Penguin Books (N.Z.) Ltd, P.O. Box 4019, Auckland 10.

SPARE RIB READER

A celebration of ten years of *Spare Rib*.

'A magazine for ladies who feel that the traditional women's magazines treat them as though they had their brains sucked out . . . It's not shrill or hysterical, neither is it smooth, sleek and totally synthetic – it's just good' – John Peel in *Disc*, 1972

'The toughest, most relevant and most likeable of feminist magazines is two years old. To reach three they're going to need funds, hope and the kind of faith that moves mountains' – Philip Oakes in the *Sunday Times*, 1974

'I used to be a Tupperware groupie – until I discovered *Spare Rib* . . . its sizzling prose blew my hibernating mind . . . and whipped up within me a passionate wish to identify with the growing sisterhood of bold, thinking women' – Val Hennessy in the *Evening Standard*, 1979

'*Spare Rib* has earned its hundredth birthday celebrations' – *Guardian*, 1980

THE FEMININE MYSTIQUE

Betty Friedan

First published in the sixties, *The Feminine Mystique* still remains a powerful and illuminating analysis of the position of women in Western society.

'Brilliantly researched, passionately argued book – a time-bomb flung into the Mom-and-Apple-Pie image . . . Out of the debris of that shattered ideal, the Woman's Liberation Movement was born' – Ann Leslie

'A controversial polemic' – *New Statesman*

'Fascinating' – *Guardian*

'Intelligently argued and persuasively written' – *Listener*

'Densely researched study' – *Evening Standard*

'An angry thoroughly documented book' – *Life*

Also published in Penguins

KITCHEN SINK, OR SWIM?

Women in the eighties – the choices

Deirdre Saunders with Jane Reed

Can we afford women's rights in the eighties?

With the economic recession and government cuts, unemployment and the dawning microchip revolution, the eighties are already a time of increasing pressure on women to give up their struggle for jobs, and relinquish the rights and opportunities hard-won over the last few decades. But *will* women (with a sigh of post-feminist relief) sink back into the job security of home-making?

Researching this Penguin Special, the authors talked to women from all over Britain across the social and economic spectrum, both outside and attached to women's movements. Here they assess the position of women, their problems and hopes. Here too, in the face of reactionary government policy and evasion tactics from all political parties, they discuss exactly why we *cannot* afford to ignore the needs and rights of women in the eighties.

WOMEN'S RIGHTS

Anna Coote and Tess Gill

'An excellent ... shot in the arm for women's equality' – wrote the *Evening News* when *Women's Rights* was first published.

This third, revised and updated edition is as comprehensive as the first. The new sections deal with changes in the law regarding Maternity Rights, Child Benefit, the plight of battered women and the Equal Pay and Sex Discrimination Acts. Much of the rest of the guide has been expanded and revised.

'Sparkling guide to women's rights' – Lord Justice Scarman

Also published in Penguins

THE SCEPTICAL FEMINIST
A philosophical enquiry
Janet Radcliffe Richards

What should feminists be fighting for?

In this important and original study, Janet Radcliffe Richards demonstrates with incisive, systematic and often unexpected arguments the precise nature of the injustice women suffer, and exposes the fallacious arguments by which it has been justified. Her analysis leads her to considerable criticism of many commonly held feminist views, but from it emerges the outline of a new and more powerful feminism which sacrifices neither rationality nor radicalism.

'A superb piece of applied philosophy, the arguments clear and cogent, the writing lucid and elegant' – *The Times Literary Supplement*

'Intellectually sober and politically practical, yet gay, witty and dashing at the same time . . . It's a model of how to write a book on *any* topic; on a contentious subject like this it's a triumph' – *Sunday Times*

WOMEN, SEX AND PORNOGRAPHY
Beatrice Faust

What do women think of pornography?

Pornography is a topic that produces feverish responses, but women's reactions until now have been left unexamined. Even the responses of the women's movement have been contradictory. In this major new work, Beatrice Faust discusses the psychology of sexual differences and how they relate to differences in the sexual and erotic styles of men and women and the influence of culture.

In a frank and polemical analysis, Beatrice Faust explores the enormous social implications of these sexual differences, from novels, films and fashion to social behaviour patterns – and rape. She argues that pornography is neither pro- nor anti-woman. But it certainly presents a misleading view of women's sexuality, and the solution is not censorship but sex education through bona fide erotica and the recognition of differences between male and female sexuality.

DUTIFUL DAUGHTERS
Women talk about their lives
Edited by Jean McCrindle and Sheila Rowbotham

'As remarkable and immediate as Oscar Lewis's *Children of Sanchez* ... an extraordinary compilation of the voices and memoirs of women over the past half century' – Emma Tennant in the *Guardian*

THE WISE WOUND
Menstruation and Everywoman
Penelope Shuttle and Peter Redgrove

'An important, brave and exciting exploration into territory that belongs to all of us, and nobody could read it without a sense of discovery' – Margaret Drabble in the *Listener*

THE AMBIVALENCE OF ABORTION
Linda Bird Francke

In interviews with men and women of all ages and social groups, Linda Bird Francke describes the human experience of abortion, and in doing so casts new light on one of the most controversial and complicated issues of our time.

HOUSEWIFE
Ann Oakley

'In an interesting, carefully researched and well-written study, Ann Oakley traces the historical development of the housewife role, examines the present-day situation of women as housewives, not only in terms of how society sees them, but more importantly, how they see themselves, an analysis dramatically illustrated by four case histories' – *Hibernia*

WORDS AND WOMEN
Language and the sexes
Casey Miller and Kate Swift

'Dear God', wrote one little girl, 'Are boys better than girls? I know you are one but try to be fair.'

George Orwell was right when he talked about the prefabricated words and metaphors – 'bitch-goddesses', 'the man-in-the-street' – that litter our everyday speech. We use them because they are convenient and easy: here the authors consider just how they affect our moral values, our religious beliefs and our attitudes towards the sexes.

SCREAM QUIETLY OR THE NEIGHBOURS WILL HEAR
Erin Pizzey

Erin Pizzey's struggle to open, and keep open, her refuge for battered wives in Chiswick has become a national issue, opening up to public scrutiny a problem that has been, hitherto, conveniently swept under the carpet.

FROM HAND TO MOUTH
Marianne Herzog

This book describes the lives of quiet desperation led by thousands of women exploited in factories.

From Hand to Mouth is an account of the experiences of Marianne Herzog and others on the production line in some West German factories which are household names – Philips, Siemens, Telefunken. Backbreaking piecework, boredom, fear of unemployment and coping with ill-health, shopping, home and family are all part of the hand-to-mouth existence of these factory workers.

PSYCHOANALYSIS AND FEMINISM
Juliet Mitchell

The author here reassesses Freudian psychoanalysis in an attempt to develop an understanding of the psychology of femininity and the ideological oppression of women.

VINDICATION OF THE RIGHTS OF WOMAN

Mary Wollstonecraft
Edited by Miriam Kramnick

Walpole described her as 'a hyena in petticoats'. Her *Vindication* was received with a mixture of outrage and enthusiasm. In an age of ferment, Mary Wollstonecraft took the prevailing egalitarian principles and dared to apply them to women.

Subsequent feminists tended to lose sight of her radical objectives, but it is a tribute to her forceful insight that they are finally returning to the arguments so passionately expressed in this remarkable book.

THREE GUINEAS

Virginia Woolf

A witty, elegant and lucid polemic which magnificently argues the case for sexual equality and for women's liberation. Far from being – as might be expected – a rarefied treatise on Bloomsbury's notions of 'literature', *Three Guineas* is an extremely pertinent and well-aimed opening shot in the battle which still rages today.

WOMAN'S ESTATE

Juliet Mitchell

In this stimulating analysis of a movement which has many links with student radicalism, hippy ideologies and Black Power, and which cuts across barriers of class and race, Juliet Mitchell discusses the central theoretical debate between feminists and Marxist-socialists on the nature of oppression.